Playful Learning

Offering an innovative and dynamic approach to adult learning, *Playful Learning* explores the potential of play in adulthood with the goal of helping educators, corporate trainers and event designers incorporate play-based activities for adults into both educational and work settings.

Through a comprehensive overview of the value of play in adulthood, this book responds to the growing popularity of playful events for adults in academic and business settings designed to promote higher levels of engagement. Drawing on the authors' own decades of experience at the forefront of the field, this helpful reference incorporates strategies and techniques for bringing play into any learning design. Examples and case studies of successful playful design at conferences, training events, and in higher education illustrate what effective playful event design looks like in practice.

With a multi-sector appeal that spans business, education and entertainment while bringing together practice and theory in an accessible manner, *Playful Learning* is a must-have resource for researchers, practitioners, managers and administrators alike.

Nicola Whitton is Director of the Durham Centre for Academic Development and Professor of Education at Durham University, UK.

Alex Moseley is a National Teaching Fellow and Head of Curriculum Enhancement at the University of Leicester's Learning Institute, UK.

Playful Learning

Events and Activities to Engage Adults

**Edited by Nicola Whitton and
Alex Moseley**

Routledge
Taylor & Francis Group

NEW YORK AND LONDON

First published 2019
by Routledge
52 Vanderbilt Avenue, New York, NY 10017

and by Routledge
2 Park Square, Milton Park, Abingdon, Oxon, OX14 4RN

Routledge is an imprint of the Taylor & Francis Group, an informa business

Library of Congress Cataloging-in-Publication Data
A catalog record for this title has been requested

ISBN: 978-1-138-49643-9 (hbk)
ISBN: 978-1-138-49644-6 (pbk)
ISBN: 978-1-351-02186-9 (ebk)

Typeset in Sabon
by Deanta Global Publishing Services, Chennai, India
Printed and bound by CPI Group (UK) Ltd, Croydon CR0 4YY

To Bernie: well played.

Contents

Figures

Tables

Case Studies

Acknowledgements

We would like to thank everyone involved in inspiring, forming and running the Playful Learning conference: the local committee, the wider review committee, the local support team at MMU, the catering staff, security, portering and technical staff: who have taken our ethos and played with it to create something amazing. To everyone who came and joined in, who tweeted and wrote about it, who complained and moaned about it. To our family, our friends and our colleagues who put up with it. Thank you.

No otters were harmed during the production of this book.

Contributor Biographies

Liz Cable is a Senior Lecturer at Leeds Trinity University with research interests in using escape games and immersive scenarios for learning and assessment.

James Charnock is Conference and Events Officer at Manchester Metropolitan University. He fell into event management 14 years ago and has been swimming in free buffet lunches ever since. He splits his time between thinly veiled organisation and utter confusion.

Giskin Day is a Principal Teaching Fellow at Imperial College London where she sometimes gives students silly things to do. She is course lead for a BSc Medical Sciences with Humanities, Philosophy and Law.

Rosie Jones is Director of Library Services and OpenLearn at the Open University. She has worked in academic libraries since 2001, taking a particular interest in games and learning, and conference games in particular, having run games at LILAC, ALTC and the Playful Learning Conference.

Mark Langan is Professor of Higher Education at Manchester Metropolitan University, a National Teaching Fellow and Principal Fellow of the Higher Education Academy. His interests include higher education metrics and teaching practices that foster creativity and empower learners.

Alex Moseley is Head of Curriculum Enhancement at the University of Leicester, a National Teaching Fellow, and Visiting Fellow at Aarhus University. He researches the role of play in learning and designs playful learning experiences for higher education and museums.

Katie Piatt is eLearning Manager at the University of Brighton and has a wealth of experience in development, implementation and evaluation. Her research focus is on creating effective methods of engagement, particularly regarding playful approaches combined with technology. Katie is a core member of the Association for Learning Technology (ALT) Playful Learning Special Interest Group and is always happy to playtest any educational activities or take the role of playmaker to keep everyone engaged.

Emily Shields is a professional librarian working in digital library systems with an abiding interest in developing and delivering playful learning training. Such is her passion for playfulness, she's swapped the traditional librarian's uniform of twinset and pearls for sparkling Dr Martens.

Andrew Walsh is an Academic Librarian, University and National Teaching Fellow based at the University of Huddersfield. He also works part-time as a trainer and writer and runs a micro-publisher of affordable books for professional development. More importantly, according to his daughter, he is a librarian who teaches grown-ups how to play.

Nicola Whitton is Director of the Durham Centre for Academic Development and Professor of Education at Durham University. She is interested in the role of play to support constructive failure in learning, and her recent research has focussed on the potential of escape room design.

David Woolley is a practicing teacher of mathematics, and he has taught across Greater Manchester in a variety of roles, from NQT to AST. He is currently a deputy headteacher at Cheadle Hulme High School and the Research Director for the Teaching School. He completed his doctorate in professional education in 2012.

Part I

Introduction

1 Introducing Playful Learning Events

Alex Moseley and Nicola Whitton

Think back to the last business, community or academic event you attended. Did you get the usual joining instructions, with bus routes and hotels? Did you arrive at a registration desk and pick up a badge bearing your name? Did you sip mediocre coffee while looking for familiar faces and avoiding others? Did you sit and listen to a talk or watch a presentation? Did you repeat these several times, before it was time to leave; and were you given an evaluation sheet to complete or that you forgot to complete?

The authors contributing to this book have done all of that, many times over. They have co-organised events that include some of those very activities: being, as most people are, constrained by venues, time, money and convention.

Introduction

Six years ago we were both travelling back from a conference, bemoaning the standard, tired format that seemed designed to quash creativity and limit time for discussion and exploration with others. We began to make a list of the things at the heart of this problem: too long to repeat here, but we are sure you could do the same based on your own experiences (start with sponsor presentations and PowerPoint bulleted lists and proceed from there). In a playful twist, we then started a thought experiment to design a conference of opposites: removing the negative aspects and replacing them with contradictory positive ones.

Over the next few years, we had the opportunity to work with many colleagues at various teaching and learning events to introduce some of our new playful principles into established conferences. Many of these colleagues have chapters in this book and share details of some of our successes and some of our failures. We, and our colleagues, learnt a lot from these experiences (particularly from the failures). In 2016, we put all of this knowledge into the design of our own 'conference of opposites', *Playful Learning*, running initially in Manchester for three years, and then moving to Leicester from 2019 for the next three. Who knows where it will end up next?

Designing Playful Experiences

Collectively, we are interested in how play, games and playfulness can benefit adult learning and educational practice. As an introduction, we cover this in detail in Chapter 2, where we focus particularly on the value of playfulness, which we describe as "a state of mind or an attitude; a willingness to accept and embrace the constraints of ... any activity, to try something new, to attempt something difficult where success is not guaranteed". Between us, we have investigated playfulness in adult learning contexts, most often in the context of higher education; but then we turned our thoughts to the wider sphere of learning events for adults in all contexts, from classroom to boardroom, and to those constraints at the root of uninspiring events.

Putting on an international conference is, as some readers will know, not a quick or easy experience; but we had a set of principles to work from, and we had a growing number of colleagues and collaborators who could build on their experiences in developing playful experiences to help us. From the outset, we adopted a playful attitude to organisation and found that we could extend that playfulness to other areas of event management (the catering staff, caretakers, technical support, and so on). Our institutional conference organiser, James Charnock, tells the story of how this intrinsic playfulness affected his own approach to event management in Chapter 3 – and describes the positive elements he now applies to other more traditional events.

James is one of a number of practitioners who have contributed to this book. In several cases, this is the first published article they have written; but they are joined by, and have collaborated with, a number of experienced academic writers. It is this supportive and authentic mix of academic and practical authors that makes this book useful and straightforward for anyone involved in any aspect of event or experience design, management and delivery.

As you flick through the chapters, you will find that this is not a traditional academic book, in the sense that is written in clear and uncomplicated language with a focus on practical advice and is therefore accessible to anyone in a business, community or education setting. However, it is academic in its rigour. All of the chapters are based on years of evidence and critical reflection, drawn from the individual and collective research and practice of the authors in and around teaching and learning events. Crucially, the authors draw on that evidence base to offer something new and exciting in learning event design and delivery.

The book is divided into six parts. The first comprises this introduction. The second contains the two chapters described earlier and focusses on the design of playful experiences. The final chapter in Part 2, by Rosie Jones and Alex Moseley, considers design from the audience perspective: carrying warning notes about assuming all audiences are the same by reflecting on the application of similar playful approaches across two different conferences.

They suggest design based on the collective outcomes (and desired behaviours) of both audience and organisers.

Creating Play Spaces

Playful design provides a good base for developing more creative and engaging events, but ideally, playfulness should flow across an event to the delivery itself to create playful learning spaces, and this is the focus of Part 3. In traditional events, we are used to the idea of the 'icebreaker': an activity to warm up an audience and get them working with the speaker or with each other. Liz Cable has been using activities like this in her own teaching and training for many years, and in Chapter 5 she shares some of her more playful 'interludes' to introduce playfulness into events, encourage collaboration and create a group ethic and to energise events through timely interventions.

Sooner or later many learning events culminate in a plenary presentation or two or break into workshops or seminars. Perhaps the most traditional parts of any event, such activities fit into standard forms that have been used for decades (in some cases, such as the plenary lecture, for centuries), and as such these may be the most difficult into which to introduce playfulness. Andrew Walsh, in Chapter 6, considers what sort of invitations might allow attendees and presenters alike to give themselves 'permission to play' in such circumstances. Once permitted, he uses his long experience as a playful trainer to suggest ways that different events (from a single teaching session to a multi-day event), and different activity types (including construction toys and the recent phenomenon of escape rooms), can lead to engaging, creative sessions.

Emily Shields is an experienced conference organiser and has been secretary to the largest UK academic libraries and information literacy conference (LILAC) for many years. We invited her to join the Playful Learning Committee, and she reflects (in Chapter 7) on how to interface playfulness in a committee for creativity, with the more serious side of working with venues, volunteers and programme management as the event runs.

Engaging Participants

At the heart of learning events, are the people who take part in them. The fourth part of this book considers different ways of engaging participants at events. There are an increasing number of game forms that break down the traditional barrier between 'in the game' and 'not in the game' (the much-debated 'magic circle of play' first suggested by Huizinga, 1955). Collectively known as *pervasive* or *immersive* games (Montola, Stenros, & Waern, 2009), such games or experiences spill out of expected spaces and interface with other spaces that non-players might inhabit. There are events that fit closely in this genre: seminars in public spaces such as libraries or museums; rural- or city-based training activities; arts events that are free-to-all; street theatre or performance; and so on. In Chapter 8, Giskin Day describes her teaching activities that create immersive experiences in central London and see her students solving mysteries across a number of public museums (while carrying balloons). Giskin talks about how her players, the public, the spaces and the puzzles bring everything together to make a highly immersive experience – and how she has dealt with problems and issues that threaten to break that immersion.

Learning events, particularly longer or larger versions, rarely stand alone as self-contained entities. In many cases there is either a requirement, or a wish, to engage with groups external to the main event: project partners, community groups, businesses, other organisations and even the general public. David Wooley is Deputy Headteacher at Cheadle Hulme High School in Manchester and worked with us over three years to integrate conference-based activities with research and development work for his sixth form pupils, culminating in the pupils designing and running a set of challenges for conference attendees throughout the event. In Chapter 9 David discusses the different challenges involved in interfacing a working school with a research conference and describes how playfulness played an important role in building confidence and agency in himself and his pupils.

The most involved example of an event is a multi-day conference: in which any of the activities and design methods described so far might play a part in the greater whole. Katie Piatt brings these elements together in Chapter 10 to draw on her own extensive practice of designing engaging whole-conference playful experiences, comparing and contrasting approaches between formal and informal events and providing practical advice for those wanting to tackle a conference-type event themselves.

Playful Practice

In the penultimate part of the book, we focus on some of the core features of playful events – large-scale lectures, use of technology and tools and evaluation, and consider how these established practices can be made playful. Jones and Moseley return to the topic of engaging activities in Chapter 11 to look in particular at the specialist form of the plenary lecture and how the tightly-constrained elements of this traditional format can lend themselves to playful disruption and building confidence in playing with the format.

Digital technology is pervasive in much event delivery, sometimes causing conflict or confusion where these do not interface well (such as a bespoke social network enforced by an event, that interferes with attendees' own choice of existing networks). It can also enhance the participants' experiences through better connectivity, socialisation, visual fidelity, and information finding. Katie Piatt tackles the technology issue in Chapter 12. She uses her experience as a leading technologist in higher education to ask first why you might use technology and then how digital approaches and non-digital tools can help to deliver challenge, collaboration and creativity.

Evaluation, on the other hand, is rarely liked by attendees (unless they have something extreme to report in complaint or praise) and is often poorly designed: meaning that the main purpose of the evaluation, to feed back into the design of future events, is hampered by poor response rates or low-value data. Mark Langan, in Chapter 13, looks at event evaluation: how do we know that an event has worked as intended, and what can we learn for next time? He considers various forms of evaluation, and how they offer different constraints and opportunities for a playful lens, to enable richer and more useful feedback for event organisers: moving on from the tired and ubiquitous 'smile sheet' or questionnaire.

The book finishes with Part 6, the conclusion, which draws on some of the key themes that have emerged throughout the chapters and considers what the future holds for playful learning practice.

Conclusion

As we mentioned previously, this is a practical book, based on real evidence from extensive practice. This approach flows through the chapters but is also augmented by the inclusion of 36 case studies, which you will find as boxed text throughout the book. Each case study describes a playful event, activity or approach, and reflects on lessons learned. Given the wide range, you will hopefully be able to find at least a handful of case studies to inspire your own learning event – regardless of topic or form.

The parts, chapters and case studies allow you to choose your own path through this book. You might have an urgent need to design a particular event and might jump straight to the most relevant chapter; you might be looking for inspiration, in which case a flick through the case studies might suffice. You might be interested in playfulness as an ethos, in which case you might begin at the beginning and explore its many forms in the context of event design.

Above all, we hope that you will be inspired to try a small change next time you train, teach, organise or run an event: to introduce playfulness into the design or delivery and see where your creativity can take you, your organising team and your learners.

Part II
Designing Playful Experiences

2 Play and Learning in Adulthood

Nicola Whitton and Alex Moseley

Introduction

Play is fundamental to human existence. It is integral to child development and learning and valuable throughout the whole of life (Bateson & Martin, 2013). Play can be a powerful force to inform, engage and influence attitudes and behaviours. It is embedded within the fabric of Western society, as playful approaches are used increasingly to engage adults in the media, workplaces, social networks and interactive technologies; or are chosen deliberately by adults to fill leisure, commuting or holiday time. There are a wide range of physical, mental and social benefits associated with play and playfulness, including sociability, cognitive development and emotional well-being (Proyer, 2011, 2013). Play allows for the creation of safe spaces for experimentation, practice, failure and learning from mistakes; it allows learning through active exploration and problem-solving; and it can create engaging, immersive and motivating learning environments (Whitton, 2014). Play can also facilitate social interaction, develop emotional resilience, stimulate creativity and imagination, support problem solving, reduce stress, and increase happiness (Lieberman, 1977; Proyer, 2014).

Despite its benefits, play in adulthood is often stigmatised, little understood and under-researched (Guitard, Ferland, & Dutil, 2005). We argue that while there are some similarities between the forms and nature of play in adulthood and childhood, adult play is fundamentally different from the play of children. Ways of playing, motivations to play, barriers to play, and effects of play differ enormously from children to adults (Colarusso, 1993), and crucially, while play in childhood is generally accepted as natural and inevitable, play in adulthood is commonly derided. With its associations of frivolity, silliness and inherent pointlessness, play in adulthood is often stigmatised, misunderstood and deprecated. This is a key difference between the play of children and adults – children play instinctively, adults make a conscious choice to play. It is very important that when we consider how to design playful events and experiences that engender learning, we make the most of the benefits of play without disengaging people. For some adults, engagement in play is a deliberate choice and statement of identity, for some play is not a consideration and for others it is deeply unsettling.

Using play and playfulness to facilitate adult learning provides a variety of benefits. By creating safe and trust-based learning communities, we can create a "magic circle of playful learning" (Whitton, 2018, p. 3) in which participants can take managed risks knowing that they can fail safely and positively and build the resilience to learn from failure rather than being put off by it. Using play enables us to make-believe and step into other worlds to try out things that would be impossible or impractical in the real world – to adopt a "lusory attitude" (Suits, 1978) or a "spirit of play" that enables us to imagine new possibilities and explore different perspectives. Play, by most definitions (see for example Caillois & Barash, 2001; Huizinga, 1955), is an intrinsically motivated activity, so people take part in play for its own sake and not for an external outcome or reward. It is participant-led, empowering learners to follow their own paths and areas of interest. Often this occurs within a bounded space (temporally, physically or the "magic circle of play-fulness" that a participant willingly enters and leaves). However, the impact of play has a wider reach: approaches, solutions, trials, stories, emotions and other elements derived through play can have a greater or lesser effect outside the magic circle, in the 'real world' beyond. Finding and creating these spaces is often the most difficult challenge within adult work, education or life.

Case Study 1: #playfote12 (Katie Piatt)

A game was commissioned for the annual Future of Technology in Education (FOTE) conference, which serves as a platform to share creative and challenging ideas about the use of technology in education within the education community. One of the keynotes focussed on the potential of games and learning, and the game aimed to exemplify this in a practical way by improving delegate engagement with the content of talks. The game made use of a leaderboard for the delegates to compete by completing questions and tasks; the main point-scoring opportunities were around a question posted for each session.

Questions and tasks were tweeted using the hashtag #playfote12, distinct from the main conference hashtag, and delegates also tagged responses and replies. Scores were recorded in a Google Spreadsheet, which added the players' points together across the elements of the game. These scores were then displayed in a leaderboard, and top scoring players were located in person and given stickers. Running software such as a leaderboard brings with it technology challenges; for example, it is important to make sure the screensaver does not kick in.

Ensure you have transparent scoring and can respond to unexpected situations fairly.

I had also requested that presenters hide images of potatoes in their slides, which, when spotted, acted as bonuses. Nearly all of the presenters put at least one potato (such as a photo of chips for a 'take-away' idea) into their slides. This added an additional layer of humour and surprise. The final element was of sabotage – physical evil 'Mr Potato Heads' were hidden around the sponsors' area and when spotted would deduct points from the current leader.

I wanted to build suspense, especially at the end of the game, so only published updates to the leaderboard every 20 mins to give it more movement and interest. This also allowed time to tweak the weighting of score elements, so the rankings changed and people felt that they were in with a chance. Around 10% of the delegates actively joined in with the game (35 out of 350). This was a very technology-heavy conference, with Twitter incredibly active and tweets relating to the game may have got lost; and the additional game layer was a distraction for some delegates. It is important to strike a balance between visibility and becoming an annoyance for non-engagers.

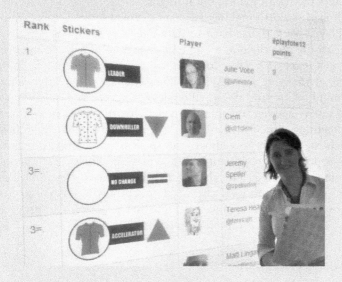

Figure 2.1 Leaderboard at the Future of Technology in Education Conference 2012.

Credit: Katie Piatt.

Games, Play and Playfulness

In this section, we will briefly examine some of the terminology associated with play, in particular exploring the differences between *games* and *play*, and between *play* and *playfulness*. Play scholars have for years been try-ing – unsuccessfully – to create a definitive definition of games and play (see Egenfeldt-Nielsen, Smith, & Tosca, 2008; or Suits, 1978 for interesting discussions on the subject), and this is not a debate we wish to enter into here. Simplistically, we define games as a form of play in which players per-form an unnecessary task, often competitive, under a set of explicit rules, where there is a clear way to measure if, and how well, that task has been completed. Play, on the other hand, is open-ended and more free-form, it may also have rules, but these tend to be implicit and mutable, and often there is no clear goal or endpoint. De Koven (1978) makes the important distinction between a game that is played to win and the game that is played to continue the joy of playing (the 'well-played game'). Games might, there-fore, have an extrinsic goal (winning the game), while play is driven by an intrinsic joy (engagement for personal amusement). In practice, there are many overlapping examples, and it is impossible to make a clear distinc-tion between games and play in all cases; in fact, English is one of the few languages that has separate words for these two ideas. Games and play are, however, different yet interrelated constructs. To engage in play does not necessarily imply the use of games, but it might.

We think it is also worth making a second distinction between *play* and *playfulness*. Play is an activity, hard to define definitively as we have dis-cussed, but generally described as an activity that is voluntary, open-ended and engaged in for its own sake, for which the key reason for playing is the enjoyment of the play activity itself. Playfulness, on the other hand, is a state of mind or an attitude; a willingness to accept and embrace the constraints of a play activity, or indeed any activity; to try something new; to attempt something difficult where success is not guaranteed. Playfulness is an approach that embraces whimsy, the spirit of the carnival, creativ-ity, humour, surprise and imagination. While play activities are commonly approached playfully, this is not always the case; take, for example, the solemnity and ritual in high-level chess. Likewise, playfulness is not lim-ited to play or games but is a state of mind that a person can apply to any activity.

Play and Games in Adult Learning

Games have the potential to support adult learning in three key areas. First, good games, by their very nature, employ good educational strategies, such as problem-based learning, collaborative learning, and experiential learn-ing. They also embody techniques for self-supported learning, such as scaf-folding, gradual increases in difficulty, and progressive hints. Second, games use a wide range of strategies for engaging players (who, after all, only play because they want to) using mechanics such as visible progression, competition, and explicit – difficult yet achievable – goals. Third, the ephemera of games (boards, cards, pieces, hardware or screen graphics) act as play signifiers, identifying the play space as separate from the real world and inviting experimentation, exploration and other playful activities that have a learning potential.

Adults engage in many different types of play. Play activities can take many forms, and we think it is useful to use an inclusive definition of play. Some play is highly structured with explicit rules, while other forms are open-ended and emergent. Some types of play are solitary, some social, some competitive, some collaborative. Play can be physical, it can be mental, based primarily on skill or based predominantly on luck. It can be silly, frivolous, comedic, but it can also be deeply serious. Play can use technology (video games), traditional tools (board games), a mixture (alternate reality games) or use no artefacts at all (I spy). In order to show the wide scope of activities that we consider as forms of play, we offer a classification in Table 2.1, which shows a variety of different types of play, with examples. We appreciate that these categories are not necessarily comprehensive; nor are they mutually exclusive. We include them here to illustrate the wide variety of activities that we consider forms of play in adulthood.

We use the term *playful learning* to describe learning approaches and activities that use play (in any of its many forms). This can include tools such as games or play activities, but most importantly, it is about embracing a spirit of playfulness that goes beyond the formal structures of adult learning and generates a mindset of possibilities that an individual can apply to any context.

The Paradox of Playful Learning

To conclude this section on games, play and playfulness, we thought it would be worth highlighting the paradox inherent in the notion of playful

Table 2.1 Different forms of play in adulthood

Type of Play	Examples
Adrenalin play	Roller coasters, extreme sports, bungee jumping.
Carnival play	Audience participation movies, zombie run.
Creative play	Sandpit play, Minecraft, LEGO, improvisation.
Exploration play	Micro-words, simulations, geocaching, treasure hunts.
Imagination play	Toys, immersive dining, role play, sex play, fancy dress.
Games	Board games, card games, video games, war games.
Performance play	Acting, karaoke, clowning, battle re-enactment.
Physical play	Team sports, free running, juggling.
Puzzles	Crosswords, quizzes, Sudoku, escape rooms.
Risky play	Gambling, drinking games, spin the bottle.

learning. Play, by definition, is a voluntary activity; if a player is forced to play, then they are, therefore, no longer playing. This question of whether an enforced learning activity can ever actually be *play* is one that many play and learning scholars struggle with, but it may be an arbitrary paradox if we consider it from the perspective of playfulness. If we consider a play activity to be simply a type of activity that people can choose to engage in (or not) as with any other endeavour, or any other learning task, then what is important is the attitude of *playfulness*, and that cannot be forced, nor restricted to play. Without an associated willingness to be playful, a play activity is just an activity. A state of playfulness cannot be coerced or imposed, but it can be encouraged and facilitated. We, as educators, can create safe spaces and trusting communities where playfulness can thrive. We might be able to compel learners to play, but we cannot make them approach an activity playfully.

Motivations to Play

There are many reasons why people play; people play games for the mental challenge, the physical challenge, the social challenge, to relieve boredom, or to provide a focus to make uncomfortable social gatherings go more smoothly. Play provides a way to escape from the flow of normal life, to be with other people in a focussed way, and to experience laughter and joy. From a biological perspective, there is evidence that play in children and animals evolved to provide a safe way for the young of a species to practice the skills that they would require in adulthood, such as hunting for food, fighting and socialisation with others (Brown & Vaughan, 2010). Play in childhood is a normal stage of human development in which children explore the world, test boundaries, learn about how things work and develop social and emotional skills (Lillemyr, 2009).

However, it is important to recognise that motivations for adults to engage in play are different from those of children. While play for most children is a natural and inevitable part of engaging with their peers, for adults it is a conscious decision, with one, or more, discernible motivations that are likely to be related both to a person's current context and to their inherent persona. As there is enormous variety in forms of play (see Table 2.1), and a huge diversity of learning contexts, there is an even larger variety of ways in which adults can engage in playful learning for a range of different reasons. Play is not a single activity but a wide spectrum. It is crucial to be aware that one person's play is another person's torture (in our case, we each view role play and karaoke very differently). Different types of people will be motivated to engage in different forms of play, at different times, and in different contexts. For playful learning to be accessible and acceptable, it is crucial that we acknowledge this.

What is key, then, in terms of designing playful learning opportunities is to recognise that not all participants will be intrinsically motivated to engage in a specific activity, but that most learners will be willing to give it a try if they recognise the value for learning in that activity (Whitton, 2007). Briefing and preparation is, therefore, key to the success of playful learning and an essential foundation for developing a playful learning community.

Case Study 2: Conundrum-Collection-Creation (Nicola Whitton)

A team-based icebreaker activity used with student groups of up to 30: students work in small teams to solve three types of challenge: puzzles (conundrum); collecting sets of things (collection); and making or designing a thing (creation). Challenges are written on cards (around 24 in total for a 30-minute game) and groups start with three cards; when they complete a challenge (with evidence), they can randomly take another card. Teams have to complete as many challenges as they can within a set time period, and the team with the most points at the end wins a prize.

This game aimed to provide a focussed – but clearly non-serious – activity for groups to engage in so that they would have to interact with one another in a light-hearted way.

Examples from a version of the game designed for a PhD student induction:

Conundrum: Wise Words

Who doesn't love a bit of educational philosophising? But do you know who is credited with the following quotes?

1 "Freedom of conscience entails more dangers than authority and despotism."
2 "Children must be taught how to think, not what to think."
3 "If the structure does not permit dialogue the structure must be changed."
4 "I believe that children are our future, teach them well and let them lead the way."

Collection: Je t'adoor

Doors are amazing, aren't they?
Create a photo collection of six different doors in this building.
You must include at least one door from every floor.
Save your favourite door until last.

Creation: Cheesy Moments

You love cheese.
You love Japanese poetry.
Write a haiku about your favourite cheese.

Versions of this game have now been used in a wide variety of settings including project inception meetings, student inductions and as conference activities. They have been generally successful at getting people working together, laughing and engaging with one another on a social level. While not wildly competitive, the inter-group competition element adds an additional layer of engagement. It is good to tailor the challenges to specific groups so that the game becomes personalised. For example, for an EU inception meeting, a number of challenges were included relating to countries in the consortium, and at a conference for library professionals, several of the questions were based around famous librarians.

Only on one occasion has a group failed to engage with the game, which happened at a research induction social event for staff and students. A small group of professors simply refused to engage at all and sat in a corner talking loudly about their research. While in this case they were ignored by the players and it did not affect the game overall (and it is important never to force anyone to play in a way that is discomforting), it is always worth considering strategies to deal with rudeness and public disengagement.

Designing Play for Adult Learning

We have already highlighted that play in adulthood is different from that of children, both in terms of its forms and motivations. In this section, we will examine some of the key aspects that need to be considered when designing playful learning events, activities or experiences for adults. We will explore the link between playfulness and learning, considerations related to the language of play, the potential of game mechanics for engagement and opportunities for playfulness at work.

Playfulness and Learning

Earlier in this chapter, we described a "magic circle of playfulness", which is at the heart of the value of play for learning. This concept of a 'magic circle' is one that game designers (drawing on Salen & Zimmerman, 2004) and play theorists (drawing on Huizinga, 1955) have used to describe the mutually-agreed play spaces (real, temporal, virtual or imaginary) in which games and playful activities take place. The magic circle does not have a hard border but is enclosed by a 'fuzzy' liminal zone (Harviainen, 2012; Remmele & Whitton, 2014) that denotes the transition between non-play and play (or real life and play). What invites a particular player to enter the magic circle and cross the border is linked strongly to their motivations to play, as we describe above. We can also make the magic circle clearer and invite through signifiers or artefacts (e.g. game pieces or graphics, ball pools or LEGO bricks, friends in a circle). A particular genre of games, *pervasive* games, such as *alternate reality* games, use the trick of making the edge of the magic circle indistinguishable from the real world. In these games, the fictional narrative intersects with reality (for instance, through a text message or newspaper advertisement from an in-game character). This encourages an integrated playful approach from the participants, who become open to, and aware of, invitations to play at any time and in any context.

If we frame playful learning events within a magic circle and make efforts to construct that magic circle as a welcoming, safe and trusting community space (through, for example, introduction activities and opportunities for participants to get to know one another beyond a superficial level), we can enable the creation of playful and open learning communities. The physical artefacts associated with games and some forms of play (e.g. playing pieces, cards, toys, playful architecture or furniture) help to signify the presence of the magic circle for players and non-players alike. In this safe space, learners can take agency over their own decisions and try new things that potentially carry a personal risk. They can be aware that they may fail but feel supported by the play community to do so and to learn from any failure that occurs. As in many forms of video game, failure is normalised and becomes an inevitable point on a path to success. Video games are designed for players to fail repeatedly, and yet this does not deter players. Failing, and learning from failure, is an integral part of the playing experience (Juul, 2013), and a game without the possibility of failure would be dismissed by most players as too easy and boring. The use of a magic circle of play allows us to embrace failure as a natural and inevitable part of a learning process; this provides the space for measured risk-taking, builds resilience and ultimately increases scope for creativity.

While playful learning embraces a set of tools and techniques for drawing participants into the magic circle, it is more than that; it is a philosophy of learning. Nørgård and colleagues (2017) present a signature pedagogy of playful learning (based in higher education but equally applicable to all forms of post-childhood education) that distinguishes between the surface structures (game tools), the deep pedagogies (play techniques) and implicit values and assumptions (a philosophy of playfulness) that underpin playful learning. It is these values of acceptance of failure, openness, democracy, willingness to try something new and willingness to enter into the spirit of play, that are the key underpinning factors in creating a successful playful learning environment.

The Language of Play

The word 'play' itself has many different meanings, not all of them associated with the positive aspects of playfulness. You can play a game, play an instrument and act in a play, but you can also play up, play the fool and play with someone's feelings. The language of play in relation to adulthood can have particularly pejorative connotations, with associations of silliness, childishness and wasting time.

Sutton-Smith (1997) highlights this ambiguity of the notion of play; identifies what he calls "seven rhetorics of play". Simply, these are: play as animal progress; child's play; play as the hands of fate and chance; play as a form of power; play as power and identity in children; play as a signifier of the imaginary; play as expression of the psychological self; and play as frivolity. This final discourse of 'play as frivolous' is perhaps of most concern to the promotion of playful learning. However, Sutton-Smith himself highlights that "frivolity, as used here, is not just the punitive negative, it is also a term to be applied more to trickster figures and fools, who were once the central and carnivalesque persons who enacted playful protest against the orders of the ordained world" (p. 11). This focus on the frivolous potential of play for disruption and reimagining, rather than for silliness or purposelessness, is more in keeping with the notion of playful learning and the ethos of this book. Indeed, play is already used as a disruptive element in modern culture – in art (see Flanagan, 2009) and in a cynical response to corporate bureaucracy (such as 'gaming' telephone call centre targets, as described by Woodcock, 2017). However, this active, critical approach is not how the public at large commonly perceives play.

People working in the field of play and learning have long used language techniques to legitimise the approach. We use terms such as 'simulation game', 'serious games', and more recently, 'serious play', to highlight the solemnity and gravitas of these forms of play, but also implying that other forms of games or play are non-serious and therefore frivolous (in its negative sense). While this language may increase the acceptability of playful approaches to wider audiences, we feel that it may also undermine the value of play by implicitly endorsing the rhetoric of frivolity. It is the very playfulness of play – its intrinsic lack of seriousness – that we believe is the basis for its learning potential. Rather than reconfiguring play as a serious act, we need to focus on the value of play and playfulness for its own sake and make sure that academics, games scholars and learning designers hear this message.

Playful Mechanics and Engagement

Game design focusses on core 'mechanics' that form the basis of gameplay and combine to make a game fun to play. These range from overarching approaches such as competition or collaboration to specific features that make a game work, such as win conditions or dice rolls. Over time, as game design has turned into the billion-pound industry it now is, designers have honed these mechanics into perfect ways to keep players engaged with a game, making them interesting from a learning perspective.

The feedback mechanic within games is a good example of this. Games use positive and negative feedback to help players understand what they need to do to improve. For example, an adventurer chopping at a door with an axe might see and hear splinters and creaks coming from a particular place on the door – indicating where they should focus their next hit. In a racing game, a player will find that the computer-controlled cars stay just ahead of them, no matter how good the player gets at driving. In both of these cases, players are encouraged to continue playing and know what they need to do. Schell (2008, p. 230) notes that feedback has a variety of functions, noting that players get "judgement, reward, instruction, encouragement and challenge" from game feedback. These functions fit readily to existing concepts in the assessment of formal learning, as Moseley (2013) found when applying them to the teaching of history.

As well as feedback, games use other design patterns that create engaging approaches in learning contexts. The way that many massive online games combine collaboration (players working in teams) and competition (teams battling against each other to move up a leaderboard) provides a model that could easily transfer to group work in adult learning. Many modern games provide 'modding' or development engines with which players can create their own levels and challenges; an approach that resonates with ideas of students-as-designers. Throughout the other chapters in this book, you will spot other mechanics drawn from popular games that were used in the development of playful approaches in events and activities.

Case Study 3: A Referencing Game (Andrew Walsh)

This game can be used with groups of up to 60 students in higher education. It aims to allow learners to practice building references using a standard system and to introduce the patterns that underlie this standard.

I found that many of my students, in common with the academic staff that teach them, are scared of referencing. They obsess over minor details and panic in case they are getting it wrong. This game allows learners to practice building references in a low-risk environment, reinforcing learning through repetition, followed by a discussion where they start to see the underlying patterns used by the referencing system.

In advance, I prepare envelopes containing each of the components (on small cards) to build a correct reference (for example, author, date, title, place of publication, publisher). I label each envelope with a number of points available (1 point for an 'easy' reference like a book, 5 points for something harder like conference proceedings). Students work in small groups to gain points by correctly completing references. They start by selecting an envelope of their choice, deciding whether to go for quick and easy references or harder references that will gain them more points. Once they have completed a reference, they can claim another envelope. They normally have a referencing guide available to allow them to copy the example formatting.

I allow them a set amount of time, and then the group with the most points wins a small prize (normally sweets). Importantly, by the end of this exercise, each group will have a set of references built in front of them. The group looks for patterns to create for themselves some general rules to follow when creating references in future. Every time I've used this, students have told me it has reduced their fear of referencing and helped them see how to reference in future.

Playfulness and Work

The majority of modern companies and institutions are focussed, to some degree at least, on metrics: whether those be sales, profits, results, impact or quality. While this is familiar territory for big corporations, adult education providers are now operating with the same aims; universities are increasingly focussed on student survey results, league tables and measures of research and teaching excellence. In these outcome-focussed, high-pressure environments, there is often very little room for play and playfulness.

This wasn't always the case. There is the famous example of Xerox Parc providing game rooms, beanbag lounges and other playful spaces for its R&D teams in the 1970s, and the eminent science researchers Fleming and Feynman both used playful methods to develop their Nobel-prize-winning work (Bateson, 2014). Many innovative technology companies, notably Microsoft and Google, are known for their playful work environments to encourage networking and creativity.

However, play in work settings is seen by many people as inappropriate and trivial, exacerbated by the conflicting and pejorative associations in the language of play, as discussed earlier. In our experience, we have found three ways to counter this viewpoint. First, it is important to prepare the ground for play. This might be a cultural or perceptual preparation (providing space in a timetable or linking play to positive outcomes), or a physical preparation of space. Huizinga (1955) and Sicart (2014) have both described physical "playgrounds" that invite play, whether through architecture, furniture or playful objects within a space. Depending on the work context, spaces might need to be in keeping with an organisational ethos, but communal social spaces are often a good place to start being playful. Second, it is crucial to create a compelling invitation to play and legitimise it in a work setting. This might be as simple as a tic-tac-toe board within a communal kitchen, or magnetic letters on a fridge, or it could be through designed invitations such as challenges issued and linked to rewards such as free coffee. Third, we can look for senior role models who authenticate play for the wider institution. Include such leaders in the development of playful spaces or activities, or demonstrate the value of play within a strategic meeting, project or other flagship event. While the opportunities for play in the workplace may be limited, we hope that this book will provide some insights into ways to legitimise and capitalise on the full benefits of play for socialisation, innovation, and creativity at work.

Conclusion

In this chapter, we have considered the pedagogic foundations for understanding the nature of playful learning, with all its potential benefits. While playful approaches to the design and implementation of events and activities clearly have advantages in terms of learning and engagement for many people, it is crucial to recognise that the ability to play is a privilege not afforded to all. In this final section, we highlight some of the barriers to play and consider ways of making play more inclusive.

Play is a privilege for those with the time, inclination, appreciation of value, the confidence to fail or look foolish in front of other people and the physical and mental abilities to engage. Certain forms of play are expensive (e.g. extreme sports), requiring economic capital; others require the social capital to engage (e.g. exclusive golf clubs, university dining societies); and others require gaming capital to engage, that is, an extensive pre-existing knowledge of the play form (e.g. role playing, cryptic crosswords). It is also important to recognise the embedded forms of privilege and power in certain forms of play that marginalise specific groups or minorities and make them less likely to engage (e.g. the representation of women and people of colour in video games) or the physical barriers to play (e.g. wheelchair access to play spaces).

While the magic circle provides a useful metaphor for thinking about the theoretical construct of a play space, it can only be an idealised construct and is inadequate to describe the messiness of the real world. It is impossible to create true safe spaces that are devoid of the power relationships of the real world (as anyone who has ever played corporate team building games with their line manager will recognise) and impossible to create real spaces with no consequence outside of the magic circle. Players are real people with personalities, emotions, relationships and rivalries that will not miraculously disappear under the auspices of play. It is important that we, as proponents of playful learning, appreciate this and recognise the limitations of the magic circle as well as its potential. When designing playful learning events or experiences it is crucial, therefore, to consider who might be excluded (for any of the reasons discussed above, and potentially more) and make a real effort to make the experience as inclusive and accessible as possible.

3 Designing Playful Events

James Charnock

Introduction

In 2015, the Playful Learning conference was conceived by three academics as an antidote to traditional conferences; moving away from didactic presentation formats and accepted forms of conference engagement to provide a platform for presenters and delegates to explore new ways of engaging people in their work. Playful Learning has now run three times, each time experimenting with the conference format, often successfully, sometimes less so – as we will discuss later.

This chapter will explore the creation and evolution of this conference from the perspective of a professional conference organiser and will use the Playful Learning conference as a case study. Playful Learning is a three-day event that aims to epitomise playfulness throughout so that playful approaches are embedded within as much of an event as is appropriate (which we will discuss later). I will look at how the conference embedded playfulness, and the difference between that fundamental ethos and 'gamification' for its own sake, with no underlying remit or purpose.

This chapter will also explore the design of playful events more generally, particularly focussing on organisations and venues that house, or financially underwrite, other conferences and events that typically take a more traditional format. First, it will describe the Playful Learning conference in detail and explore how its ethos makes it different from other conferences; it will then examine how to get buy-in from a range of stakeholders and how to cater for a range of different attitudes to play in an event audience.

I will consider different attitudes to play and risk at every level. Looking at it from a host organisation's perceptions of 'playful' activity and the perceived reputational risk, and considering different types of delegates and their perceptions of play. Attitudes to play and risk may differ greatly and be dependent on context and experience, from delegates' previous exposure to playful learning to their positions in an organisation (and therefore the amount that they can be seen to 'play' or accept play as an appropriate method of learning). I will also look at the relationship between an event organiser and client, both in terms of explaining the nature of playful events to an audience who may have no prior knowledge of them, and in fostering a relationship between the two where playfulness begins to be introduced by the host institution as well as the event organisers.

This chapter focusses on the 'big picture' design, planning, and institutional considerations of putting together any playful event, but is particularly relevant to large, externally-focussed events. Alongside this, consideration of the day-to-day running of playful events is given in Chapter 7.

Case Study 4: Sea You, See Me (Giskin Day)

This activity was a pick-up-and-play, seaside-themed, tabletop team game, made available to delegates at the Playful Learning Conference in 2016. It aimed to help participants at a playful conference get to know each other by giving teams of two to five players silly things to do for about 15 minutes of playing time.

Each game was packed in a small bucket that players could pick up from the conference registration desk. The bucket contained a series of short activities, introduced through consecutive prompts given in an envelope, a fish-and-chips packet, a recycled small bottle, and on a seaside postcard. The first instruction was in an envelope marked 'Start here', and players were instructed to only open the other elements when prompted to do so. The game started with participants each revealing a secret word on a homemade scratchcard. They were challenged to drop their word (e.g. 'cucumber' or 'hedgehog') into conversation three times before the end of the game without their fellow players being able to guess it. The next prompt was to tip out the contents of the bucket, which included fake sand, shells and cocktail umbrellas, to set up a mini beach scene. The following activity (given in a fish-and-chips packet) was to have everyone place a cellophane 'fortune-telling fish' on their palms. Depending on the way the fish curled up, participants were allocated a famous person to pretend to be (e.g. 'moving head' – the Queen, 'moving tail' – Elvis). There were some scripted prompts to read out in the style of the celebrity. These challenged participants to make up some game rules on the spot for some imaginary, difficult-to-pronounce games. Further prompts had participants seeing who could blow a whirligig for longest using a single breath, making a mini-sandcastle, mixing up some artificial snow and making it 'snow' on the 'beach' for a chance to reminisce about favourite cold-weather games before bringing the game to a close by guessing each other's secret words.

This is a game that is easy to overcomplicate with too many props and prompts. It can also work as a paired activity, and it can be adapted for different settings by tailoring the conversational prompts to the theme of the conference.

Figure 3.1 Playing 'Sea You, Sea Me' at the Playful Learning conference.
Credit: Playful Learning Conference by Mark Power.

Playful Learning: A Conference with a Difference

The annual Playful Learning Conference is an event that began at Manchester Metropolitan University in 2016 as an alternative to more traditional conferences of its type. I have been working in the conference and events industry for over 14 years now, and even at the start of my career, there was discussion in the field about the limitations and pitfalls of the traditional conference format. We know that traditional conferences are not always an effective way to network and share information, yet the model is still propagated.

It is true that some conferences are experimenting with more radical approaches, such as unconferences, which are loosely-structured events that typically focus on discussion and networking, but may also be difficult to obtain funding for in university systems that recognise traditional research outputs. There is also a middle ground, where many of the original ideas of 'the conference' are revisited to bring their essential worth back to the fore. For example, in PechaKucha, 20 images are each displayed for 20 seconds, forcing the presenter to talk with brevity and pace about their ideas. The essential format of a conference presentation is still relevant, but the new constraints force delegates to reconsider how to present their ideas most effectively.

Playful Learning builds on this idea of using a variation of alternative and traditional formats to get presenters to rethink their practices and create a space where those involved in research, teaching and learning and study in the field of play can meet to learn and create together, but also play and experiment. The conference takes place over a reasonably traditional format of three days of workshops, presentations and keynote speeches. However, within that, there are almost constant opportunities to play and network. Delegates are encouraged to explore engagement with play, take steps beyond their boundaries to try something new, and experiment with risk and failure, primarily in the name of furthering the possibilities of a playful approach to learning and play for adults. They are given the opportunity to subvert traditional conference formats and try new approaches. I believe there is also an emergent secondary goal of empowering delegates to feel as though they can try anything, leave their comfort zones and become more rounded practitioners by exploring what they find difficult, rather than repeating things they find easy.

For many academics, the motivations for running a conference are to provide an academic arena in which to present papers to peers, which may also lead to a formal publication; to make contacts and network; and to promote the work of the host and subject discipline. The motivations for attending a conference might be to present work and get feedback from peers, to learn about the state-of-the-art in the field, to network with colleagues and to be inspired by the keynote speakers at a more holistic, 'big idea' level. Playful learning is different because it actively encourages presenters and delegates to play with the form and practice of the conference in a playful manner, so that delegates become part of a playful community, shaping and defining the conference as it emerges. Learning and sharing are at the core of the conference, and motivations go beyond the traditional; most of the delegates come in equal parts to present, share and learn.

The philosophy of Playful Learning has five pillars, which underpin all of the activity within the conference.

- **Innovation.** The conference has a visceral, emergent feel, supporting fresh thinking and innovation – maybe not even tried and tested. This extends into the approach the conference has to failure, which is that it is to be supported, celebrated and viewed as a learning experience.
- **Integrity.** Being ethical, fair, inclusive and open in procedures and policies is key to the ethos of the conference. For example, we operate at-cost to keep prices low and the conference accessible, all keynotes receive the same token payment or charitable donation, we encourage new keynote talent and we have operated for the last two years as a vegetarian conference in an effort to reduce carbon overheads.

- **Rigour.** The subject nature of the Playful Learning conference is inherently subject to greater scrutiny than other 'more serious' subject areas, so ensuring the quality and robustness of the conference is crucial. All contributions are double-blind peer-reviewed, and we have a high rejection rate; alongside that, the conference committee provides a mentoring process to support potential presenters with good ideas to meet high levels of academic rigour.
- **Mischief.** Underpinning the conference is a genuine sense of fun and playfulness, with a sense of disruption and subversion. We aim to provide an environment where delegates can embrace uncertainty, be surprised, try new things, be actively engaged and be silly.
- **Collegiality.** My favourite of the pillars, encapsulating the willingness of participants to engage with each other and share their ideas, successes and failures.

There is an almost palpable sense that there is philosophical buy-in for these pillars by the community, along with a sense that experimentation and failure are hugely important and will be treated as entirely positive.

The Sessions

The presentations take a wide variety of formats, from the more traditional presentations (although almost always subverted in some manner) to seminars and workshops. Most of the delegate contributions are hands-on or discursive, and presenters can contribute using the spaces in any way they can imagine (health and safety allowing). In previous years this has included a storytelling tent, the 'ghost of Hamlet' roaming the conference venue and a make-your-own-video-game arcade.

The Keynotes

Our keynotes are drawn from a range of disciplines that cross the realms of education and play research. These have included artists who work with pervasive gaming and experiential public events, experts in play and transformational change, as well as experts from within academia. There is also an additional focus on our explicit equality agenda to ensure that, for instance, the gender inequality in education, tech and conference speakers is not just addressed, but rebalanced for the better.

Fringe Fun

Fringe events have helped (re)shape the conference each year. There has been a growth in elements that sit outside, but complement, the core conference programme, including the student escape room project (see Chapter 9), where local school students are invited to demonstrate their escape rooms during the conference as well as attend the keynote and other sessions that day. This provides a sense of a 'once in a lifetime' opportunity to playtest original escape room ideas, creates a counterpoint to the academic sessions taking place across the day and gives delegates another means of networking with each other.

One of my very favourite things about Playful Learning is its attitude to creating spaces for networking and sharing ideas. I have helped organise many more traditional conferences where every paper is of very high quality, where every exhibitor has been appropriate and worthwhile, but where the networking opportunities boil down to plucking up the courage to sidle up to another delegate at break or lunch and tentatively say hello. Often a great deal of thought has gone into creating spaces to network, without any discussion as to how people who do not know each other are going to use these spaces to their best advantage. We are people. Some of us are good at saying hello, some are not. The ability for people to be together to collaborate and share is crucial to creating value for a physical conference in a digital age. Putting people into a frame of mind where this is not just possible, but efficient and deeply meaningful, is something that Playful Learning has done well since its inception, and a large part of that comes down to creating spaces where this happens organically, not expressly labelled as networking.

Two of the best (and simplest) of these are:

Routes into registration. In the Brooks Building, which has been Playful Learning's home for its first three years, 99% of conferences locate their registration desk adjacent to the main doors of the building. In Playful Learning's first year, we hid it. This meant that delegates had to come in, immediately engage with the conference game (see Chapter 10), have their photo taken (see Figure 3.2) and begin talking to each other, if only to share in the initial unusualness of the experience. This was then compounded at registration, where they weren't simply given a pack and told when the first session was, they were invited to take part in a game designed to foster networking at random (none of which was expressly labelled with the dreaded moniker 'icebreaker').

Free play. The common areas of the conference are filled with giant versions of traditional games, which provide not only a lovely backdrop for our photographer to go to town but also a very low-key, simple way for delegates to interact, with enough of a shared goal and area of interest. We are also lucky enough to have had access to a project that gave delegates the chance to play on some arcade machine emulators, featuring classics like Donkey Kong and Pac-Man. Here again, the emphasis is not on the individual, but on a shared interest, through which networking can naturally occur. I have watched delegates interact over the board games or arcade game emulators; they have space and time to relax in each other's company and then embark on more pointed collaborative activity; or not, as the case may be. The point is about creating opportunities for interaction that are organic and not forced, and there are loads of them at Playful Learning.

Figure 3.2 Playmaker photographs delegates during conference registration.
Credit: Playful Learning Conference by Mark Power.

Playing with Food

Aside from the temperature of the rooms, the major subject of feedback from the majority of conferences and events is food. The food that should be provided at a conference is the subject of much debate, but this ability to create debate and bring people together is often ignored. Playful Learning asks you to challenge yourself. Each year we have given as much thought to our food offering as to any other element of the event, to ensure that the ethos of the five pillars extends to delegates' choices at lunchtime. In the second year of the event, we decided to make our most common dietary requirement, vegetarian options, into the focus of the catering, offering only non-meat options for every meal. This provoked innovation from the catering team, helped the environment and gave vegetarian delegates a much-appreciated opportunity to enjoy more than the traditional stuffed pepper that is so regularly thrust in front of them. Changing the focus of our meal times from catering to the masses to asking people to explore a new set of possibilities inspired debate, outbursts of joy from the minority group usually asking for the alternative option and even led to some recipe swapping as people were enlightened as to the possibilities of the humble vegetable.

An important point here is finding the balance of an idea like this: during the discussions for the 2018 conference, we considered going a step further and making the event completely vegan. However, after much debate and some initial canvassing of opinion, we decided that this may be a bridge too far for some, who were happy to explore being vegetarian for a couple of days but saw veganism as something beyond their comfort zone.

Playing with Signs

Embedding playfulness throughout an event is important, and one example of how to do this is through playful signage, which can surprise and delight but must also be usable. Take for example the maps that we use to help delegates move around our buildings, which are a complicated collection of rooms based on the original plans of the space. For Playful Learning, we stripped this right back to simply show the rooms, common areas and the social spaces delegates would be using, thus making it much easier to understand and navigate. This template was then themed around the conference, using the structure of a level of Pac-Man to introduce a nod to play, but also a framework that virtually all delegates, based on their demographics and interests, would be likely to identify with and understand (see Figure 3.3).

Beyond the aesthetics of a design like this, it is also an unspoken call to action. That is to challenge delegates to get around this space using vocabulary from the game.

Playful Feedback

Feedback as a whole is discussed much more in Chapter 13, but here I explore the process I have been through in the last three years in terms of moving from a position where I was used to producing traditional feedback forms to a place where the mechanisms we use are possibly too outlandish. In the years that come, I think we will move back to a place where we can, through the trial and error of the last three years, make feedback as themed, fun and 'different' as possible, while also ensuring it is a meaningful, informative process that yields feedback of real value.

In the first year of Playful Learning, the committee was, if anything, against any kind of traditional feedback process, quite rightly declaring the 'happy

Figure 3.3 Playful conference signage.

Credit: Playful Learning Conference by Mark Power.

sheet' a box-ticking exercise with no meaning or future use. However, from my position in the institutional conference organisation team, I have a wider requirement to get feedback not just for the conference, but for the service areas I cover, to ensure that we can continuously improve on our offer and celebrate success when we do things right. I believe fervently in the power of feedback if done correctly, so reframing this, like so many other areas of the traditional conference, has become a minor obsession of mine.

To meet in the middle, and bearing in mind that the conference and its audience were new to me at the time, I decided to create feedback forms that had a playful element. As a result, the Aeroplane Feedback form was created. If folded correctly, it gave delegates the chance to complete a fairly conventional set of questions, but with the bonus that it could also be coloured in and 'flown' into a basket (the 'feedbasket') at the front of the stage. This created a challenge element, which was clearly embraced, given the 92% feedback rate (compared to the 20% response rate we get using our usual feedback forms).

That said, there were still issues with plane-based feedback, as I witnessed delegates, desperate to be the first to throw their planes (in some cases redesigned, clearly we ignited a schoolyard desire to create the 'best flier') almost immediately. This had the knock-on effect that some of the forms were hastily, and only partially, completed, which may have given the whole ethos of the feedback process a very literal 'throw away' feel; but at least the forms were completed. It is also worth mentioning that if I know one thing about feedback, it is that people pushed for time immediately, and emotively, write down their gut reaction to an experience – the thing that they've loved or hated the most, and the collated data reflects that.

By year three, and with a pirate theme for the conference, I decided to theme the feedback mechanism even more. After consultation with the committee, we agreed on making the feedback form into a parchment, with the same questions (so that we could compare data year on year) translated into pirate parlay. When delegates had completed the form, they could roll it up and put it in a (small recycled plastic) bottle. The initial idea was that these would then be deposited in a paddling pool, left to float, aesthetically beautiful, as a last act of the conference. In the end, they were thrown at me while I sang 'Message in a Bottle', accompanying myself on the guitar. Some days I really earn my money. As amusing as this was though, I realised partially at the time, and definitely with the hindsight of reading the feedback, that the wording of the questions was so 'pirate-y', and therefore open to interpretation, that many people either reacted badly to (yet more) pirate puns or misinterpreted the question in my desire to fully 'pirate' the questionnaire. This has meant that some of the positive and negative responses have been blurred through over-theming the mechanism, resulting in a loss of validity of the responses.

But the process has been immeasurably helpful. There is no innovation without an overstepping of the boundaries. Now I know exactly where to pitch the feedback.

Case Study 5: Society of Musical Legends and Children's Television Heroes (Nicola Whitton)

A conference dinner icebreaker game, used on the first night of the first Playful Learning Conference in 2016. It aimed to get conference delegates to speak to new people and move around during the meal, to avoid people sticking to established friendship groups and increase inclusivity.

On entering the venue for the conference dinner, each delegate was randomly given a card welcoming them to the inaugural dinner of the Society of Musical Legends and Children's Television Heroes, and telling them their identity for the evening. All delegates were either members of a famous band or a classic children's TV series. Their first task was to create a customised name badge and find the other members of their band or series (in case participants did not know who they were, the invitation reminded them: "Please feel free to Google yourself if you have forgotten who you are. We do not judge you.")

Figure 3.4 A typically creative entry to the 'concept album' challenge.
Credit: Arjan van Houwelingen.

Delegates then sat with their group for dinner and worked on the second challenge: to tweet a team selfie to re-launch their careers as the group reform. After the main course, each group was given a second envelope containing their third challenge: to join forces with another group to create a concept album.

Each group was provided with an album cover template and various craft materials to create their albums. At the end of the evening, each album was presented to the other participants. The levels of creativity and humour were amazing. Overall, feedback from the activity was very positive, with delegates saying that they appreciated the effort to get people to talk to one another.

Getting Buy-In for a Playful Event

Making playful events possible is, theoretically, reasonably simple: choose a venue based on its suitability for your sessions and opportunities to let delegates connect; marry that with a backroom staff who understand the event's ethos; and if the sessions are strong enough, you are sorted.

The reality is sometimes a little different. The core ethos of Playful Learning took me some time to understand, and even though I knew right away that I believed in its message, I still made mistakes. These boil down to assumptions about, for instance, what 'play' means in this context, how academically rigorous it is despite the outwardly, at times, frivolous appearance, and how far removed it is from other, what I thought were similar ideas, such as mindfulness and gamification.

Getting a real understanding of a conference's core principles is one of the chief ways in which a conference organiser creates trust with the academic organisers of the conference (along with doing what you've said you'll do in a timely fashion). I view it as my role to be someone who understands the subject of an event thoroughly and can translate that into something that other stakeholders (e.g. security, catering), who have no other stake in the conference beyond getting their area right, can understand.

A lesson I have learnt from Playful Learning is that if you can explain and educate these disparate groups in the ethos of a conference, you end up with a team who buy into the conference's vision and even begin participating where appropriate. Translating the ideas of a group of academics into something operational teams can understand and use, while also gradually getting them on board with why we are doing what we are doing, is a rewarding challenge. An example of this gatekeeper role would be in the first year of Playful Learning, when one of the organisers ran into trouble with the catering team, who controlled the usage of space in our dining room. The organiser needed access to part of the space that had been screened off by the catering staff. The organiser did not understand why they could not access *their* space, and the catering team would not let them use it, because it would affect set up of a later part of the conference. In effect, both parties were working to the same end, but it is an example of a breakdown of communication that led the organiser to a perception of 'difficult' staff, and staff having a perception of 'difficult' organisers. In the end, the academic got to use the space, understanding that the staff were just 'doing their jobs', and I explained to the catering team that sometimes, academics are all deeply unhinged.

Overcoming assumptions is really key to getting the most out of the venue you choose to have an event in. Convincing 'services areas' such as food, buildings and accommodation, as well as perhaps other core users of the building, of what we mean by play and how to be playful. Playful Learning, perhaps more so than other conferences, encourages a blurring of the lines and welcomes everyone to take part in play whatever their role, so, for example, catering staff have actively taken part in challenges and as competition judges.

It is important to take time to explain to all stakeholders the ideas you have for an event and their benefits in simplistic terms. This is not to suggest that we offer operational staff a 'dumbed down' explanation of Playful Learning that in any way reflects their perceived ability to understand it, more that this is not their area of expertise and they are busy people. The connotations of the word 'play', for example, for people not involved in the area, come with a whole set of preconceptions about the amount of mess, disruption, noise and generally 'silliness' involved in an event. A lot of it also boils down to the organisers of the event treating the policies and procedures of the venue with as much reverence as they expect service area staff to treat an idea that they hold dear – trust on both sides. Having a giant sandpit in the middle of an atrium may well be possible with four months' notice, buy-in from all building users and a risk assessment completed but mentioning it 48 hours before the event will solicit a very different response.

From a design perspective, when trying to convey your requirements to service areas, keep it simple, visual and practical. On one level, venue set-up staff just need to know where objects go and what risk there is to them being there, not necessarily what they represent and why it will change the face of playful research forever. On the flip side, however, a greater knowledge of why something is being set up or is taking place where it is brings with it a greater likelihood that staff will buy into it, or better, suggest possible enhancements, or be able to add value in other ways.

In my experience, diagrams are always better than a verbal explanation, and certainly better than reams of emails explaining where something will go 'in relation to that bit of the stairs next to the large red chair'. It is always worth remembering that what is 'The Conference Game' to person A is a table and two chairs to person B. In the three years of Playful Learning, it has been really nice to see the gradual way staff members have worked out what the conference is all about and then started adding value by suggesting playful elements that organisers may be unaware of. For example, themed food that we've included in the event, from lunchtime refreshments including customised buns to a vegan street food catering offer, which jointly helped us experiment with enhancing our sustainability offer while supporting the pillars on which Playful Learning stands. We've also collaborated with our sports department to allow delegates to try neon badminton (think *Tron*), rave fitness and, in keeping with the pirate theme of the last conference, fencing.

Using the facilities of a large university may initially look easier than using a stand-alone venue with no other connected departments, but that is not necessarily true. Convincing other stakeholders around the university to collaborate across departmental boundaries and embrace an event where the outcomes benefit all parties is actually quite tricky in a large institution *because* it is a large institution. Stand-alone venues may well have partner organisations, repeat clients or links to the local community where these 'specialist' tie-ins can be found. This has knock-on benefits of providing a wider audience for an event and extending the possibilities to consider social responsibility.

Convincing senior stakeholders, particularly in a large organisation, that an event like this is worthwhile is also important to consider. From a financial perspective, clearly, it is key that an event achieves whatever marker is set out for it, whether that be breaking even and therefore being self-sufficient, or providing a contribution to the institution that has agreed to put its name to it. There is also reputational risk to consider, and in a wider higher educational sense, this is almost more important.

Considering the impact of national and institutional metrics, and how fast misappropriation of resources could go viral these days, it is obviously important that there is buy-in from all levels, and that social media is used appropriately and with an understanding of how an uncontextualised message might be viewed. During the second year of the conference, for instance, I tweeted a desire not to work with the organisers anymore due to their 'frankly absurd requests'. It was obvious (to me and the organisers at least) that this was in jest, but not to the wider public, which in this instance included a senior member of the university management. I subsequently deleted the tweet and learnt a valuable lesson about audience and social media reach.

It is also worth mentioning the benefits that events like Playful Learning bring to venues. The nature of some of the activities (such as the large visible board games) means that a conventional venue gets turned into an aesthetic dream ripe for photography, publicity and social media impact.

Case Study 6: Hashtag Hunt (Liz Cable)

This is a variation on a Scavenger hunt played using social media tools. We played it on Vine, Twitter and Storify, but it could be run using most forms of social media.

It was a group-building activity designed to introduce the concept of the hashtag as a tool for curation and community. Everyone playing could identify each other online and follow, so it wasn't just groups working together, but all participants would be connected, demonstrating how hashtags can be used as community-building tools while creating a community of learners.

A hashtag was created for a photo-taking challenge, and all teams had to respond (either correctly or creatively) to a series of prompts. Teams posted their photos or videos to the social media platform with their team-name hashtag, the challenge hashtag and the hashtag of the event. After a while, new challenges started popping up on the hashtags, including some that were aimed at particular teams. Players had learnt to monitor the platforms and set up hashtag searches, as well as respond to comments and challenges aimed at them.

It worked really well as a device for teaching hashtags and as a way for the players to have fun getting to know each other. It could easily be adapted for an induction or exploration activity.

It is worth considering that if a longer-term record of an activity is required, a platform-agnostic version at the end of the activity needs to be created. Both the digital tools we used – Vine and Storify – have since gone offline, and our content has disappeared with them. It is important to be aware of the ephemeral nature of some platforms – especially the free ones we tend to utilise for this sort of activity. It is also crucial to ensure the hashtag you want to use is not already in use for another purpose before you start.

Designing Inclusive Playful Events

Playful Learning is designed to be inclusive and democratic, and it is crucial to recognise that not everyone plays, or is playful, in the same way. Creating opportunities to play, or to sit back at times, is at the heart of designing playful events. It is important to prepare delegates for play. I initially assumed that the core demographic for a conference of this type would know what to expect in terms of the levels of engagement, participation and boundary-stretching they would be asked to do, but the first year taught me that there are a lot of people involved in this area of research and practice who still find this approach as new and scary as I did.

The cultural mix and expectations at an event like this are also worth mentioning. In year one, I sat at dinner with two Italian delegates who were almost offended at having to take part in an activity over dinner. Whether this was age, nationality or a mixture of the two, it is worth remembering that many people do not want to play all the time. People need downtime and markers that, when asked to push back boundaries, can still form a target where they know they can find some downtime and 'normality'. This is especially relevant at an intensive three-day conference; spaces where it is OK not to play, or pause from play, are important.

It is crucial to recognise diversity in motivation and potential for engagement in an audience and to cater to as many people as possible. From my experience across many conferences, any audience will be made up of people with one of five broad underlying attitudes to play at a given time (and any given individual may change attitude in different contexts depending on mood).

- **The Explorers.** The 'will do anything' people, who are up for novelty and challenge simply because it is there.
- **The Scientists.** Those people who will be willing to engage, often wholeheartedly, as long as they have a clear and evidenced rationale for taking part.
- **The Sceptics.** Those people who can be convinced to take part in a playful activity but may do so grudgingly and are often not keen. Sometimes they surprise themselves.
- **The Apathetics.** Those people who go through the motions with little or no engagement or sit at the sidelines looking pained.
- **The Curmudgeons.** The people who will not engage in play at any cost, showing their disapproval by actively disengaging (e.g. loud sighs, folded arms, walking out).

I include this rough typology not as a way of pigeonholing individuals but of getting readers to consider the potential mix of playful engagement at an event. Of course, the nature of the event will influence the mix – I would argue that the Playful Learning conference has a much higher mix of Explorers and Scientists than many more traditional serious conferences. However, what is important is to recognise this diversity and consider ways of catering for all of the different attitudes to play.

There is a range of ways in which this can be achieved, both at the level of a whole event and an individual session. For example:

- Set clear expectations and ground rules for the event so that people know what they are signing up for and that they know that there are different ways to play.
- When designing the range of activities available, make sure that there is something for everyone at different times (e.g. avoid putting all the very playful events on at the same time).

- Make the more outlandish or challenging sessions optional add-ons.
- Provide opportunities for downtime and reflection built into the main programme so that they are seen as normal and acceptable (i.e. give people permission not to play).
- Provide justifications for using playful approaches using clear briefing and debriefing for activities.
- Consider how non-engaging players might try to subvert a session and build it into your planning.

Above all, creating an open, safe and democratic conference community will enable delegates to play as much – or as little – as they want to.

Conclusion

This chapter has explored some of the big picture issues that occur when planning and designing a large-scale playful event such as a conference. What is key throughout is the value of open communication, a shared vision and a respect for different positions, skills, motivations and attitudes among stakeholders and delegates.

Obviously, there are risks associated with any playful event: reputational damage, non-engagement from participants, health and safety, developing cliques and creating the conference the committee wants to run rather than the one that the delegates want to attend. However, I believe that one of the biggest risks is *not being playful enough* in an audience of predominantly playful people who are constantly involved in that arena. There is a safety to most traditional conferences and events, where delegates know what to expect, and while they possibly deride it, actually enjoy knowing what they are getting. At the heart of Playful Learning we ask everyone – from support staff, to senior management, to delegates – to step out of their comfort zones and try something new. Sometimes they will fail, but that's OK. And I've learned more about the design of conferences in general from these steps into the unknown.

4 Play for Different Audiences

Rosie Jones and Alex Moseley

Introduction

While organised events tend to share a similar formula, for example, programme shape and layout of rooms, we have found that the audiences that attend bring different expectations and exhibit different behaviours. Playful approaches can be inhibited by preconceived notions of what an event looks like, the sense that a delegate is either a 'customer' or part of a community and the topic of the event. A conference looking at creativity or innovation is likely to suggest a different attitude towards interactions compared to a conference in a specific scientific field.

Despite these challenges, we will show that playful approaches provide opportunities to enhance traditional event experiences and allow participants to come away with extra information, connections and outcomes. If participants are encouraged to come to terms with accepting new approaches to agendas and programmes, they can begin to adopt a playful attitude. Positive behaviours such as innovation and creativity can then be encouraged by implementing other playful elements within the event.

To realise this approach, we need to consider the key elements described above. We will start by looking at the audience for which the event is being prepared. We will then consider what encourages that audience to participate playfully: the invitation. Finally, we will consider the behaviours that event organisers want to promote, the objectives that attendees want to achieve and consider how to design playful approaches that meet these with positive outcomes for both the audience and the organiser.

Case Study 7: ALTC 2015 Robots (Rosie Jones/Alex Moseley)

The Robot Game was run over the course of a three-day conference with approximately 350 delegates working in a range of roles related to learning technology, primarily higher education. The game aimed to get participants to talk to one another, demonstrate a range of game-based approaches, encourage positive behaviours among delegates such as engaging with exhibitors or asking questions in sessions and provide playful elements to the conference as a demonstration of the power of play.

The game used an overarching narrative where the evil robot DarkBot (@botofevil on Twitter) was trying to take over the world using poor quality learning technology, and delegates needed to help defeat him by choosing a robot champion to challenge him and helping that champion by completing a variety of tasks. Four giant robot posters outside the main auditorium showed the four mighty robot champions. Different rewards used throughout the game encouraged both competition and collaboration. The main playful activities were:

- Before the conference, delegates were encouraged to network by using a template to tweet what they were looking forward to or who they wanted to meet at the conference.
- At registration, delegates were given a networking bingo card, which also assigned them to one of four robot champions.
- Throughout the conference, delegates were given sticker rewards for various positive behaviours, which could be used to fill in all the sticker spaces on their team's giant robot poster, creating a visual scoring system.

Figure 4.1 Robot piñata aftermath at ALTC15.
Credit: Rosie Jones.

- In the exhibition, a loyalty card was used to encourage visits to sponsor stands.
- During the conference meal, origami hat templates and decorations were provided on each table, and the first four tables to post a picture of everyone wearing their hats were given extra wine.

While engagement with the different activities was mixed, the game created a buzz throughout the entire conference. However, the final 'epic robot battle' was somewhat underwhelming, with a small robot piñata lowered over a balcony to a small waiting crowd below. The sweet rewards that emerged also made quite a mess on the floor, which did not go down too well with the cleaning staff (see Figure 4.1).

Audience

Identifying and understanding how an audience may or may not respond is an important first step when thinking about adopting playful approaches at an event. From the experience of the ALTC and LILAC case studies (Case Studies 7, 8 and 9), it can clearly be seen that there are different levels of 'readiness' of an audience to be playful. We learnt a valuable lesson at LILAC 2016 when we attempted an almost direct replication of the game we'd designed and run for ALTC 2015 (albeit with a different theme: detectives rather than robots) and experienced low engagement and even rejection by the majority of delegates. It was evident that for an audience mainly made up of information and library professionals, the approach and activities we had designed were unclear or confusing for the attendees, who in turn saw them as too risky or confusing to engage with – particularly the more immersive narratives. Yet the learning-technology-focussed audience for ALTC had found the activities and narrative perfectly acceptable, and either engaged or enjoyed watching others engage, as we discovered from the active social media discussions. At LILAC 2016, a few attendees did engage, and in fact, engaged to a high level; but many others found it difficult to step into this playful space, particularly the more immersive narrative elements.

In hindsight, we should have repeated the playtests we ran prior to ALTC 2015 for the replicated LILAC game: we might then have identified this difference in engagement early enough to revise the design. In reality, LILAC 2016 became a playtest that failed, and this led to a downscaling and redesign of playful activities for LILAC 2017: as can be seen in the case study, this allowed for easier entry to activities and a greater ability to dip in and out of the games. Crucially for the LILAC audience, it was not essential to get immersed in or even know about the whole narrative, nor was it essential to do anything in sequence.

Case Study 8: LILAC 2016 Detectives (Rosie Jones)

This conference game ran over the course of the three-day Librarians Information Literacy Annual Conference (LILAC), with approximately 300 delegates working in a range of roles in libraries, primarily higher education. New attendees to this long-running conference sometimes commented that it was hard to network because of well-established cliques. The playful elements described here aimed to encourage positive behaviours and open up networking.

As a practitioners' conference, many sessions explored engagement within library teaching; the game was also an opportunity to investigate the application of playful techniques to teaching practice.

At registration, 'human bingo' cards were handed out, containing characteristics that had to be linked to other delegates to encourage conversation. The random colour of the bingo cards automatically put delegates into one of four teams. Each team had a blank detective poster that needed to be filled with stickers to 'win' the game.

Stickers could be won by asking questions in a session, speaking to sponsors or just at the whim of a committee member. Twitter was used

Figure 4.2 Detective posters at LILAC16.
Credit: Rosie Jones.

throughout with team hashtags (e.g. #greenPI, #redPI) to help create a team spirit and move the game along. The culmination was a piñata that the first team to complete their detective with stickers got to destroy.

While most delegates engaged with the game to some degree, interest in getting stickers waned over the three days and only a small percentage saw the game through to the end. At evaluation, we received some negative comments about 'playing' at work. We felt we could have explained more clearly to delegates the application of playfulness to their own practice and the point of the activities. Some day-delegates commented that they were confused about the 'rules' and felt slightly excluded, as by day two the teams seemed fairly established.

Invitation to Play

The reticence or refusal of the majority of the LILAC 2016 audience to engage with playful elements, and the subsequent change in emphasis and increased engagement in 2017, suggests that the pitch, or offer, of playfulness is important to understand, and is different for different audiences.

In both cases, the activities were inviting delegates to play, but in the first case the invitation was largely ignored, spurned or rejected. In the second case, the invitation was accepted. Same audience, different invitation, different outcome. From a design perspective, we, therefore, need to design the 'invitation to play' at an event. Taken at an individual level, the likelihood that any one delegate might decide to take up an activity is likely to be a complex issue: does it fit with their own expectations of the event, have they done something like it before, are their friends/colleagues partaking, are they hungry/thirsty, did they have a good journey: we could go on. Ultimately, the individual delegate will give themselves 'permission to play' (discussed in detail in Chapter 6) or will not.

When considering a group of delegates, or an event audience, those individual complexities are magnified tens or hundreds of times. As shown in the differing responses of the audience at ALTC 2015 and LILAC 2016, the audiences might tend towards a shared response that might come from a shared identity, ethos or behaviour that matches the subject or identity of the event itself (the audience at an environmental awareness conference are likely to reject any activities that go against that ethos, for example, even if individually they might have been mildly interested in the activity).

We, therefore, think that the design of playful activities, and the invitation they offer, needs to talk to the themes and needs of the event itself, and therefore of the attending audience. In the next section we'll consider the needs of both the event and the audience as *outcomes*; and for the event organisers, those outcomes might also depend on *behaviours* they want their audience to exhibit.

Behaviours and Outcomes

In Table 4.1, we have listed the most common time-bound stages of an event, from pre-arrival to post-departure. For each stage, we have then considered the most common behaviours and outcomes desired by event organisers and by the event audience. In some cases, these align well (such as having engaged participants); in others they may differ (the organisers wanting to rebook happy exhibitors vs. the audience needing particular information).

For the ALTC 2015 and LILAC 2016 conference games discussed above, we designed our playful activities to promote five positive conference behaviours – from both the organiser and attendee perspective, which are shown in Table 4.2.

This was the first time we approached the design of a playful event in this way, and we found that it was both well-received by the organisers and also increased their desire to support the activities we designed.

Table 4.1 Behaviours and outcomes for each stage of an event

Event Stages (these might be fluid and stretch across stages at different events)	Behaviour or outcome objectives for organiser	Behaviour or outcome objectives for audience
Pre-arrival/preparation *e.g. logistics, personal objectives, travelling*	Set appropriate expectations of event. Positive promotion of event. Inclusion of online delegates.	Deciding what to bring. Setting personal objectives. Exploring programme. Finding out about other delegates.
Arrival/orientation *e.g. networking, programme, landscape*	Orientation of delegates to event venue and general locale.	Meeting new people. Identifying common interests. Creating a personal programme/choosing sessions or activities. Exploring the venue or local area.
Formal programme/ sessions *e.g. plenaries/ lectures, workshops, discussions, formal activities*	Collaborative interaction within sessions. Engaged participants, arriving on time and asking questions.	Personal interaction with the topic. Meeting expectations for the session. Progressing personal objectives within the session.
Informal programme/ other activities *e.g. exhibitors, posters/ demonstrations, informal activities*	Happy exhibitors willing to sponsor future events.	Engaging with additional information and widening understanding.

Social events *e.g. formal meals, informal meals/ refreshments, trips, social activities*	Generate positive atmosphere. Develop a community.	Networking and making connections. Taking opportunity to reflect, relax and have fun.
Departure *e.g. evaluation, immediate reflection, closure*	Ideas for improvement and changes to future events. Feedback for sponsors/ funders.	Taking opportunity to reflect. Maintaining connections.
Post-departure *e.g. reflection, application*	Wider impact.	Knowing how to apply to own practice. Applying to own practice.

Table 4.2 Behaviours and outcomes identified for ALTC 2015 and LILAC 2016

Event Stages	*Behaviour or outcome objectives for organiser*	*Behaviour or outcome objectives for audience*
Pre-arrival/preparation	–	Getting the most out of the conference by preparing themselves and setting personal objectives.
Arrival/orientation	–	Making the most of opportunities to network especially with new people.
Informal programme/ other activities	Engagement with the exhibitors.	Knowing when to relax and reflect.
Formal programme/ sessions	Attending sessions on time and asking pertinent and useful questions at the end of a session.	

Case Study 9: Playful Interventions at ALTC 2016 and LILAC 2017 (Rosie Jones)

A series of playful interventions took place over the course of two three-day conferences in 2017, both attracting approximately 400 delegates. The Library and Information Literacy Association Conference (LILAC) focusses on the field of information literacy and attracts mainly librarians but also academics, learning technologists primarily from the HE sector. The Association for Learning Technology Conference (ALTC) focusses on learning technology and attracting delegates from a wide range of roles in learning technology, primarily in the FE and HE sectors.

These interactions aimed to provide opportunities for delegates to take away playful ideas and resources for re-use in their own practice, demonstrate a number of game-based approaches, and encourage positive delegate behaviours. A programme of playful interactions was dispersed throughout the conference from pre-conference to departure. Information on activities was included in the programme, tweeted or available on the conference websites.

Pre-conference activities:

- Provision of printable speech bubbles allowed delegates to interact on Twitter and identify some of their interests ahead of the conference.
- Twitter travel games using the conference hashtag for delegates as they travelled to the conference to encourage early interaction and engagement with other delegates. One particularly successful game was to tweet images containing the conference colour, and this led to both creating excitement and promoting the conference.

Activities at the conference:

- Networking cards were given to delegates in the first plenary session. During the conference, they were encouraged to try and make at least five new contacts; on the back of the card they filled in memorable connections, professional and personal.
- Like coffee shop loyalty cards, each exhibitor had a different design of stamp, which they would use to stamp delegates' cards when they visited their stands; completed cards could be exchanged for prizes.
- A model of a fictional city was created by delegates as an example of how a modern city could be connected, collaborative and creative. Delegates were able to add their own paths, building, landscapes and services, or augment others' ideas, using a variety of craft materials (see Figure 4.3).
- Small teams were able to take part in a mobile tour and quiz. Prizes were given for the quickest and most creative team.
- At the conference dinner, delegates were asked to create and augment origami hats; prizes (of bottles of wine) were awarded to the fastest tables.

Post-conference:

- Delegates created their own Twitter travel games to play on the way back from the conference.

Figure 4.3 Collaboratively re-imagining the city.
Credit: Rosie Jones.

The optional element was more successful in terms of numbers engaging than previous immersive conference games. Delegates felt more comfortable opting in and out and less like they were missing out or too late to join in. However, without clear and tangible rewards, some of the playful interactions were not used; in particular, the networking card was not engaged with well.

Designing the Approach

When designing and evaluating events, the traditional formula is usually seen as the success criteria: enough choice of parallel sessions, venue selection, catering, in fact, anything that might appear on a typical evaluation form. As we have described above, a more useful approach for both organisers and attendees might be to consider behaviours and objectives as both design and evaluation criteria. We have suggested some common behaviours and objectives in Table 4.1, but you might identify others for your own context (these could be professional work or research objectives, more general positive behaviours or objectives relating to a particular award or certificate). If the design is based on these outcomes, it is then much easier to apply playful approaches that encourage and support such requirements. As an example, if an event needs to encourage teamwork, then a playful challenge that involves collective problem-solving could support this behaviour more efficiently (and with greater attendee engagement) than a coffee/networking break could, and in a much more memorable way.

The design of playful approaches needs to be adapted to different audiences. From the case studies, it is evident that there are distinct differences in readiness to engage and adopt depending on the profile and experience of a group. This does not mean you cannot develop an audience's approach, but it is important not to discourage them with something too extreme too soon: a sure way to disengage groups who are not comfortable with the approach. Personal and group 'permission to play' is worth considering for your context – it can never be an exact science, but you will be able to identify general ideals and expectations drawn from the event topic, previous audience behaviours, sector norms, etc. You might also identify the willingness of an audience to experiment or attempt new approaches; a more conservative audience might suggest that you introduce smaller, optional approaches that test the willingness of your audience to engage.

A logical approach is to start small with playful approaches that are obviously linked to behavioural outcomes, for instance, orientation to or at the venue. A playful activity to help with orientation could be applied to any type of event and would help to set a friendly, open relationship between the organisers and participants. However, the overtness of playfulness becomes an important decision to make and will influence how well the activity is adopted: asking attendees to create name badges on arrival could involve them giving themselves Top Trumps-style ratings for key discipline skills (low playfulness), could involve them decorating their name badge with pictures, stickers and pens to represent their interests (medium playfulness) or might ask them to combine both of these approaches and also create name badges for each other (high playfulness). All three options allow attendees to share something about their interests or skills that will help when meeting each other, yet only one might be appropriate for your event. A fully immersive and abstract approach such as we took at the ALTC 2015 conference (with a pack of playful items and immediate placement into a robot team) worked for that audience but was not as well adopted at LILAC 2016 even though we had changed the theme to a more appropriate (or so we thought) detective theme. If we had started each event with a more gentle activity of limited playfulness, we would have been able to gauge uptake and introduced more immersive playful elements as the conference progressed.

Table 4.3 details the playful approaches we designed against particular behaviours, with a high level of playfulness (ALTC 2015 and LILAC 2016)

Table 4.3 Comparison of playful approaches across four large conferences

Behaviours	ALTC 2015 and LILAC 2016 (immersive narrative)	ALTC 2016 and LILAC 2017 (pick and mix approach)
Preparing and setting objectives	Delegates tweeted what they were looking forward to or who they wanted to meet at the conference.	Speech bubble activities to show aims and interests. Twitter travel games.
Networking	Delegates were given a networking bingo card that also assigned them to a team.	Networking cards given out in first lecture with activity to create five connections – no teams assigned. Optional Actionbound quiz.
Engaging with exhibitors	A loyalty card was used to visit exhibitors rewarded with team stickers.	Loyalty card only.
Engaging with sessions	Delegates were given team sticker rewards for turning up early or asking questions.	None.
Relaxing and reflecting	Origami hat at the conference meal.	Fictional city installation created over whole conference. Origami activity at the meal. Twitter travel games on departure.

and then a low level (ALTC 2016 and LILAC 2017), demonstrating alternative approaches for each behaviour.

The main change between the two conference years was the optionality of the conference game. While some of the activities may appear similar, the ALTC 2015 and LILAC 2016 activities all linked back to an overarching narrative for the game. The narrative for both of these was overtly fictional, respectively an evil robot and villain: each threatening to ruin the conference. Delegates won stickers to power up their team's robot or detective champion to go into battle with the evil character. All activities had some link into this plot, and it was clear from engagement at both events that participants found it difficult to opt in and out of the game. For ALTC 2016 and LILAC 2017, we made the activities standalone, allowing people to easily engage with whatever appealed to them, with no knowledge of the wider activities or a storyline needed. For instance, the networking activity was unchanged between the two versions, but in the earlier (immersive) version the card we supplied also put delegates into teams and allowed them to score points for their team, which was crucial to driving the narrative. In both cases, engagement with the exhibitors increased, pleasing the exhibitors and organisers.

Playtesting ideas before the event itself, with a diverse range of people, can indicate whether the desired behavioural outcome will be met. It is important that the playtests involve a range of people, including those who might embrace new or active approaches and those who would not. Identifying 'local teams' (those in the event organising committee, representing the venue, or representing the attendees) and involving them in the design, testing and implementation of your activities is hugely beneficial (as explored in more detail in Chapter 7). Local teams can offer a diversity of the more confident and the more reluctant; they allow complexity to be tested and the willingness of testers to engage with each particular element. Playtests almost always show that initial designs are too complex and that you need to simplify your approach. Involving local teams in playtesting can also help to push the boundaries, as they are more likely to allow normal 'rules' and features of an event to be bent to enhance your playful activity if they get on board with the objectives and approach at an early stage.

No matter how complex your playful design, it is important to view it in two stages. The complete design can be set in advance of the conference, following adjustments as a result of playtesting. But it is important to be responsive to the audience live, as they play, and to have alternatives and contingencies ready to respond to audience behaviour. Having a core set of initial activities, backed up by a bank of playful activities you can easily introduce as the event progresses, is one way to achieve this. Another, simpler approach, is to design the experience in a 'pick and mix' approach, where most activities are prepared in advance and available at pre-set times, but the audience is free to choose the time and nature of their engagement. In either case, being responsive to the live game allows you the flexibility to respond to reaction and adoption in the context of the way the audience is engaging with the wider event. You may also find that some participants try to subvert the game, adding elements or 'cheating' on aspects, and you can respond to this by altering the game to outwit them or allow the subversion to add an interesting variable to the event and promote it positively.

Taking the 'live' running of a game further, you can include an element that encourages and allows participants to create their own activities or challenges within your game. This might include creating missions for other attendees, issuing whole-conference challenges, or similar, and they provide both agency to the audience and also an easy way for the game to self-respond to the needs and interests of that audience. If you find that the game as you designed it originally is completed quickly by the audience, this option provides a way to extend the game live and to capture the audience's engagement. This audience-created approach also gives delegates a chance to apply what they are learning at the event and to create reusable objects that they may take back to their own place of work. At both ALTC and LILAC, sessions were run to encourage attendees to develop their own activities and, post-conference, delegates were encouraged to create new games from them. This approach can help to build ideas for future conferences and can give participants confidence to try new activities of their own.

Conclusion

We learnt an important lesson from our involvement in these four conferences over the space of two years. While our design approach for the first (ALTC 2015) was strong and considered outcomes and behaviours from the organisers' perspective to good effect, our failure to consider the context and needs of the audience caused problems when the same approach was transferred to a different context.

We, therefore, changed our approach to design for ALTC 2016 and LILAC 2017 to consider both audience and organiser outcomes and behaviours, and through this sequence of events, we have derived a set of important lessons.

Lesson 1: Know your audience (and get the invitation right). While it might be tempting to assume that event audiences follow a similar homogenous pattern, this cannot be assumed. The anticipated behaviours and objectives, and expected outcomes, of your audience are vital to understanding how they will respond to your playful activities. Of particular importance is the *invitation* you make: put yourself in their shoes (or better still, involve them in the design) to create an invitation that is both engaging and makes sense to the audience.

Lesson 2: Know your organisers. Any activities you design will need to be accepted by, or at least approved by, the wider event committee or by sponsors/funders. If you have any influence in these areas, involve the organisers and (if possible) a sample of the audience into your playful planning. The use of playfulness in an organising committee is discussed in more detail in Chapter 7.

Lesson 3: Design and test. Use playful co-design methods to boost creativity and set design aims to meet both organiser and attendee outcomes. Test any designs in advance, with a sample of the audience (ideal, but difficult) or with colleagues or the design team itself.

Lesson 4: Design-in-play. See the real-life implementation as a further playtest. This prepares you to design-in-play and to use live feedback from the audience and organisers to reflect, change, reduce or extend your activities as the event progresses. It's a good idea to hold regular meetings of the playful design team – maybe at lunch and evening of each day – and to keep in touch via a closed channel to make quick decisions and changes (text/phone/WhatsApp/Slack or similar).

Lesson 5: Learn from your failures. No activity is ever worthless: remember that by designing to desired outcomes, you are attempting to improve the experience for both audiences and organisers. As long as you learn from any minor or major 'failures', you're always improving things. By examining our failures and designing around them, we developed:

- The idea of 'toning down' the invitation to include all delegates.
- A more explicit linking of activities to learning/behaviours.
- An awareness that an invitation is always optional: choosing not to take part in something is an important outcome to design for.

We also learnt that 'success' is not always defined by the number of active participants. Success should be set against outcomes: if one of your activities fails to work, yet prompts deep discussion amongst the audience, it might have met a desired outcome of greater networking.

We hope that these lessons help you to shorten the process from 'failure' to 'success' that we experienced and have encouraged you to think about the needs and desired outcomes of your own events and audiences and how these might benefit from a playful approach to design and delivery. Our most important lesson of all is that none of the four events detailed in this chapter – whether they worked 'successfully' or not – were a waste of our time; on the contrary, the audiences, organisers and ourselves gained a huge amount of benefit from them: and a stronger sense of what makes a successful playful event for future audiences. We, therefore, encourage you to have a go with your next event: you will definitely learn something from it.

Part III
Creating Playful Spaces

5   Playful Interludes

Liz Cable

Introduction

Icebreakers are an expected part of learning events. The familiar 'give your name and tell two truths and one lie about yourself' comes from the long-running TV series *What's My Line?*, which first went on air in 1950. Considering their longevity and ubiquity, there is a lack of research around the effectiveness and appropriateness of icebreakers (Whitton, 2005). Some common variations are so outdated that they break modern cultural taboos, especially around considerations of neurodiversity. It has been common for facilitators and trainers to talk about 'forcing' participants into doing something – usually to socialise – in order for an event to progress successfully. This is no longer appropriate.

Icebreakers are very different for adult professionals than they are for, say, university students. There comes an age and stage at which adults can be expected, and will expect to be able, to introduce themselves. Arriving at an event that all participants have chosen to attend implies a level of trust and willingness that means time should not be wasted on icebreakers aimed at simply introducing participants. In the context of the playful event, we are more concerned with what it is that the participants need to know about each other to get the most out of the event, and how this can be established swiftly at the start.

It is important to take into account both the nature of the audience and the desired outcomes of the event before choosing an activity. Icebreakers are dreaded by some participants, and the wrong activity can lead to feelings of isolation and a reluctance or refusal to participate fully. This is especially crucial in an event where a playful attitude is a desired mindset for subsequent activities. Some people hear the word 'icebreaker' and inwardly cringe. The creeping doom of the invitation to 'say something clever about yourself', far from creating a friendly atmosphere of trust and openness, sends some participants into a spiral of panic. Thinking about your own experiences, I would guess it's as easy to recall bad experiences with icebreakers as good ones.

Very little research has been done on the value of icebreakers, and yet they are something, love them or loathe them, we have been conditioned to expect as part of any training course or conference. The right exercise, introduced and used in the right way, can work to improve an experience and outputs but must be as carefully planned as the rest of the content. A facilitator cannot afford for a ten-minute exercise to put off even one person from participating for the rest of the day. This is doubly true if participants are asked to leave their comfort zones to bring a playful mindset to the fore. It is important to make sure the atmosphere and environment is safe for everyone. Every activity should be inclusive and equitable by default.

There are many times during the course of an event when the tone needs to change, the group needs to focus, the energy needs to be lifted, or introductions need to be made – if only by the session leaders. So 'icebreakers', traditionally meant to break the ice at the start of the day, are jumbled up with 'energisers' and 'group-builders' or what I, collectively, will call interludes.

Types of Playful Interlude

Interludes are different from conference games (see Chapter 10). While conference games are designed to weave in and around all sessions continuously, interludes can stand alone and bring the event theme into focus in different ways. They are each an individual invitation to participate and be playful and are designed to bring the whole group, or teams within the group, together to create an atmosphere in which experimentation, play, failure and learning can take place.

Here I am going to discuss four types of interlude that can be used to break up the business of the day to get people interacting and engaging or re-engaging at crucial intervals:

1 The icebreaker or introduction, which is usually the first participatory activity for delegates.
2 The group-builder, which is designed to help groups form quickly.
3 The energiser, which happens after a lunch break or long task.
4 Parting ways (Eggleston & Smith, 2004), which brings the event to the conclusion, and celebrates what has been achieved.

This latter type of interlude can be combined with a playful assessment or evaluation activity (see Chapter 13), alongside giving thanks to the hosts and organisers, to end an event on a high note. These four activities can be linked and in fact can work together as a playful path through an otherwise traditional event. At around ten to 20 minutes each, this will be 30 to 60 minutes well spent on developing and bringing together the community of attendees.

Icebreakers

Breaking the ice refers to warming up the atmosphere and creating an atmosphere for delegates to get the most out of an event. Once the housekeeping and administration is out of the way and everyone knows when lunch is and where to get it, their attention turns to: 'what will I get out of the day?', 'what do they expect of me?' and 'will I feel comfortable here?' All very good questions that can be answered in part by an icebreaker that sets the tone and pace for the event. A good activity will allow the participants to get to know each other (or at least a group of attendees), introduce the subject and allow a little playfulness into the room. It needs to take place within safe, defined boundaries. We all know the tried, trusted and really quite bland icebreaker that asks delegates to pair up and ask each other rote questions, however wacky the questions are; it is a safe and unstimulating activity. Better to use this opportunity to raise expectations, give permission for playfulness and inject some fun.

Before choosing an activity, consider the nature of the community as it exists before you start and how/if you want the cohesion produced by the event to end. Do the delegates already know each other or do they need introductions? Is the icebreaker the forming of a team for the day, or will the delegates go their separate ways straight afterwards? Perhaps the whole event is to bring an existing team together, or an emerging team, an ongoing workgroup or community. The nature of an event's community will influence the style of icebreaker. It is important to consider what the outcomes of the day are expected to be: problem-solving, creating, learning? Is the nature of the expected participation reflective or vivacious? The icebreaker sets these expectations.

Asking participants to 'be playful' can be met with the same inner groan as announcing a 'fun icebreaker', so setting the tone, making the space safe, and modelling expected behaviour are all vital components of the introductions phase of a playful conference. Ensuring every activity is part of a learning journey and articulating this relevance alongside any additional purpose will enable participants to focus on what is needed from them and choose to participate as much as they want. Participants must be allowed to choose when and how much they participate. It is important not to justify any activity with 'it forces them to interact/speak to each other/move about'. There may be many reasons why people cannot or do not participate in individual activities that have nothing to do with them not being willing to engage overall with the learning or problem-solving theme of the day. It is the role of the facilitator to help participants feel safe to take risks, or to allow them to manage participation without excluding themselves, for example by taking an observation and feedback role if they do not want to take part in a particular activity,

The job of the facilitator is to model behaviour and join in where appropriate. When a facilitator gets involved rather than standing off, this can make the participants more at ease (Kavanagh, Clark-Murphy, & Wood, 2011) and helps create an environment where participants feel more 'at home' (Oliver & Weinswig, 1996). However, this does not necessarily mean that the facilitator joins in alongside participants, but that they demonstrate and encourage while being open about their own experiences. The aim of an icebreaker is to make everyone feel welcome and part of a collaborative community as soon as possible, so conversation and learning can be free-flowing with no fear of awkwardness. At a playful event, we are extending the additional invitation to play, to be a little silly, to know that this is a playground where eccentricity and failure is celebrated, where the process is sometimes more important than the outcome and where fun can be practiced as laughter or as deep engagement. We want participants to set aside their usual "front stage" selves (E. Goffman, 1959) and allow a peek behind the scenes, we want them to engage that sense of wonder they may have left behind in childhood.

Group-Builders

The aim of a group-builder is to bring disparate folk together as a team for a more meaningful activity or discussion to come later. The activity should give plenty of opportunity for conversation so that introductions will be incidental and made along the way. Memory-making and shared experience are key here, allowing the group to develop their own common references, in-jokes and shorthand. The facilitator should find or design an activity that enables the team to create something together that is unique to them. Be aware that if each group is asked to attempt the same task (e.g. build the tallest structure from straws and marshmallows), this will result in an element of competition between groups. If the group is asked to respond to a brief creatively, with no definite win state, this allows for much more playful interpretations and a sense of group identity to form and be displayed in the artefact created. Ideally, we want to create some sense of 'them and us' in order for groups to form, but not so much that teams feel they could fail or be judged on the result. The taking part is what is important, and including everyone in the process is the goal. This is very much about the group identity, and the whole making more than the sum of its parts, so self-disclosure should not be an expected part of the activity.

Examples of group-builders include:

- Building tasks, e.g. with LEGO, random stationery, straws or marshmallows.
- Tabletop escape games, with inter-group competition.
- Co-operative games, where the winning state is only achieved if everyone in the group wins.
- Creative tasks responding to a brief that leads into the later activity.

Energisers

Energisers are activities that change the energy in the room by re-engaging individual participants. This might be needed after a serious subject, a deep reflection or simply to get through the post-lunch lull. Energisers can warm-up the brain and the body, perhaps in order to segue into a new topic or reconnect with a topic after a break. They provide an opportunity to refocus on the purpose of the day, or to clear the decks in order to bring in a new point of view. Energisers require some kind of movement ideally, or if that is not possible, some sort of kinaesthetic activity where items are moved around team tables.

Energisers after lunch can benefit from the room being rearranged. Puzzles and activities can be placed around the room, on the walls or on separate tables. Teams can see how many items on a table they can complete or have a set amount of time on each table as they move between them. One variant is to play 'Runaround', based on the '80s TV show of the same name, where three or four options are given and participants move to the part of the room that is labelled to match their answer. This is a good icebreaker too, allowing people to see quickly what they have in common with other participants. A variant has participants place themselves in line according to their opinions on something. Marmite is a good starting point – although there may be a big gap in the middle of this line – then moving on to questions more related to the topics of the day.

Parting Ways

Parting ways comes at the end of an event. It should allow everyone to reflect on the experience and share their thoughts and action plans with other delegates if they want to. It is usually a whole conference activity and generally leads into the final activity, which is to thank the speakers and give feedback. The aim is to deepen learning and cement intentions – including intentions to stay in touch with other delegates. It is important to give people the opportunity to speak if they want to; to let people say what they feel needs to be said. The event has become what the participants made it and belongs to them now.

At the Playful Learning conferences, responding to feedback prompts and then throwing responses on balled up paper, paper aeroplanes and even messages in bottles worked very well both to liven up the room and ensure the maximum amount of feedback was given. A suitably rowdy end to the day.

Designing Playful Interludes

In his seminal paper, Tuckman (1965) reviews group development activities in order to establish his 'Forming, Storming, Norming and Performing' model of team development over time. He suggests that the length of time a group is together does not affect the progress through the model and in fact can happen in as little as a day, and that these activities take one of two forms, social or task-based, an important distinction to remember when we are asking groups to participate together. It is not necessary for a group that is only together for a day to build deep relationships based on sharing of personal information; all that is needed is enough trust for a sense of safety and belonging to evolve, however temporary.

In practice, this means considering tasks that have a focus outside of the individual. Introductions could still take place, but instead of asking about favourite TV shows or something unusual that most people do not know about you, it could be more useful to focus the questions on the reasons the participants are here, what they hope to get from the day and who they are hoping to meet.

Case Study 10: Something-in-Common Name Badges (Giskin Day)

This short activity was used as a workshop icebreaker as a fun way for delegates to get to know each other's names and to work out to which team they had been assigned for later activities.

This activity was inspired by the card game Doddle, in which two players compete to be the first to spot the common symbol in pairs of illustrated cards. Each name badge was decorated in advance with seven different stickers, but only delegates assigned to the same team had an identical sticker in common. Delegates circulated, inspecting each other's name badges, until they had worked out which stickers were duplicated and therefore which team they were on (see Figure 5.1).

To run this activity, you need a lot of stickers, with as many duplicates of stickers as you have teams. Stick the team stickers on the labels first to avoid getting hopelessly confused.

Figure 5.1 Examples of something-in-common name badges.
Credit: Giskin Day.

Planning Activities

When designing or choosing activities, it is useful to think of what you are aiming to achieve in each case. All of these are valid outcomes for interludes:

• Introduce the subject matter for the day or for the session.
• Ask participants to bring to share what they already know.
• Create teams, and help them identify skill-sets and/or roles.
• Raise energy and have fun.
• Increase motivation and engagement.
• Establish a sense of community (especially if you want this to last after the event).
• Set a shared purpose and some expectations for the day.
• Reduce anxiety and awkwardness.
• Create a shared experience and give participants something to talk about.
• Reflect, debrief and provide an opportunity to give feedback.

Consider how to design the physical environment to encourage play. Coloured paper and pens on the tables, mascots or 'team-name' cards, random items to discuss or comment on will help conversations start and encourage people not to just sit down at a table and pull out their phones. Appeal to creativity and curiosity: sealed envelopes or locked boxes, Play-Doh or LEGO. Having music playing can both set the theme and tone and signal that it is time to come together when the music stops. Playful does not necessarily mean unstructured.

Before the Event

With the aid of digital and social media tools, it is possible to start breaking the ice with participants online before an event. This is also useful in setting a playful tone and introducing the conference organisers and facilitators as well as fellow participants. Social media profiles and hashtags make it easy to start a conversation and a community before people even arrive at the event. A simple activity close to the subject matter or theme allows participants to contribute, introduce themselves through their social media bios and participate by linking to resources that are not necessarily their own. Participants can create their own content or curate other people's content, alongside micro-participations such as liking, sharing and commenting to join in. Latecomers can scroll quickly through hashtags to catch up on the discussion and introduce themselves to other conference attendees. This can be done at any point before, during or after the conference, providing a group-authored insight into the personal experiences of an event's delegates and a shared stream of memories that can be further curated after the event. It is a way for attendees (and non-attendees) to start following the right accounts to get the most out of the conference on the back-channel.

Case Study 11: Toy Trouble (Giskin Day/Rosie Jones)

A three-day conference game for the Playful Learning conference in Manchester in 2017 that aimed to promote a playful atmosphere throughout the conference. Delegates were emailed before the conference inviting them to bring along a toy companion and to set up a Twitter account for them.

On arrival, toys received their own conference packs, which included a 'mission card' and a badge on which to collect stickers for completing missions. Some missions involved card swapping (e.g. 'Give this card to the toy with the best hair. Take one of their cards in return'). Others involved taking photos or making things that they showed to staff on the registration desk to earn stickers for their badge. Once completed, mission cards were traded for new missions. Cards circulated throughout the conference, and missions were also improvised by registration-desk staff. At the end of the conference, prizes were handed out for the most mission stickers and for amusing tweets. Toys were treated to their own events, including a keynote lecture (see Figure 5.2).

Engagement with the game was excellent. An unintended consequence of the game was that tweeting from toy accounts was very popular. Feedback indicated that those delegates who used Twitter in their professional capacities found it very liberating to be able to tweet from their toy accounts in a playful way that they would have hesitated to do from their own accounts. Toy 'selfies' from conference sessions were also popular, helping to boost Twitter traffic for the conference. Using just one hashtag for the main conference (#playlearn17) and toy activity helped create a sense of cohesion through the conference.

Figure 5.2 Toys await the arrival of Professor Prod Eagle for the keynote lecture.
Credit: Playful Learning Conference by Mark Power.

The Playful Learning conference had toy mascots with their own Twitter accounts tweeting before the event one year and a simple swapping of (terrible) pirate jokes on Twitter the next. The key with both activities as playful interludes is that there was no judgement of the individuals involved. People can respond more warmly to a mascot or a joke than they may feel they can about a person; think about how dog-walkers strike up conversations entirely surrounding their pets. However, unlike dog-walking, which requires you to own or have access to a dog to take part, these two introductory threads had very low barriers to entry: a stuffed toy or a googled pirate joke. Anybody could join in, and any judgement was reserved for the corniest joke or the cutest cuddly toy. People were not required to put any real part of themselves 'out there' and be judged accordingly, which reduced the fear of participation. Equally, there is very low risk in *not* being involved. It is just a socialisation activity, and delegates can catch up online later.

Interludes During an Event

Once the participants are physically present together, the back-channel can continue throughout an event, and different types of interlude can be introduced to help the event flow and get the participants comfortable in each situation. Activities to avoid include:

- Physical games where participants are expected to touch each other or move inside each other's personal space.
- Getting participants to rely on quick wits in public as a way of introduction.
- Anything with too serious a sense of competition.
- Forcing participants to reveal personal information about themselves.
- Anything that has no opt-out.

Also be wary of activities involving physical coordination and dexterity, for example 'Catch the Ball', an icebreaker that involves passing a ball in order to learn names. This can be very stressful for people with diagnosed conditions such as dyspraxia and autism, and those who just label themselves 'not good at sports'.

Depending on the cultural background of participants, event organisers need to consider not only the aspects of physical contact required by a chosen activity, but also eye contact. These are also important considerations of neurodiversity among the participants. Nearly one in ten adults suffer from social anxiety (and a third of these take ten years to get a diagnosis), so you can almost guarantee there is one or more in any large group – and maybe more so if the group consists of those whose job roles suggest a predisposition towards autonomy, analysis or lone working.

Centre the activity on a task. Give participants the opportunity to show, not tell. Is it really necessary for everyone to know each other's names?

If so, use name badges, and let people introduce themselves through an activity rather than making introductions the activity itself. Revealing something intimate, yet within social norms is very stressful for some, as is being expected to process and remember a series of 30-second introductions. Instead, let everyone introduce themselves naturally as a task progresses. Give them something to talk about other than themselves, as well as a structure allowing them to talk as much or as little as they feel comfortable.

Secrets and Spies: A Conference Icebreaker

In this section, I will describe a conference icebreaker designed for the Playful Learning Conference in 2017 as an in-depth case study to demonstrate the key points of this chapter. Secrets and Spies was a casual collaborative escape game with elements of social deduction that was originally designed as an evening icebreaker to accompany a buffet meal on the first night of the multi-day conference. The game is, by its very nature, a secret, so players can opt in by way of a simple set of entry puzzles – a coded menu – and can climb the ranks by finding secrets, unmasking spies and solving puzzles. The players start off in competition solving problems in groups, but discover by Act 3 that they need to work together to save the world. See Case Study 12 for an overview, before I continue with further detail.

Case Study 12: Secrets and Spies (Liz Cable)

An evening icebreaker, including dinner, on the first evening of a three-day conference. The setting was a pub, which had been completely taken over by the conference. This game aimed to introduce conference delegates to each other, allow people to choose how much they got involved (or to simply sit back), and demonstrate puzzles for educational escape games.

Forty-eight different puzzles based on a spy theme were designed to sit naturally in the pub; when each was solved, it gave a piece of a logic puzzle allowing the players to collaboratively unmask the Double Agent. Some were simply tiny caches, or puzzle boxes that had to be found and opened. We also had lots of codes and ciphers in the books, and boxes with combination code padlocks. The pictures and fittings in the pub became part of the puzzles, and there were several that required collecting many pieces, some of which were hidden inside other puzzle boxes.

Teams were formed early in the evening when people took on secret identities and played a simple game involving code phrases and secret signals to identify other members. This provided a good opportunity to interact with strangers while setting a tone of slightly silly play; exactly what the conference was aiming for. The game was in three phases: find your secret identity and your teammates, find and crack the spymaster's puzzles and codes (but leave them as you found them), and finally team up to solve all the clues together (see Figure 5.3). In play, the second phase didn't last very long; players began swapping puzzles with each other (but not the answers) early on.

Some people chose to play by helping others solve puzzles but not use their own secret identity. As the game was designed to just fit into the setting, people who just wanted to sit in the pub and eat and drink could do so. Ensuring every table had pieces of different multi-part puzzles meant that every group had somewhere to start. People who had never played an escape game worked alongside very experienced players to share the victory. It created shared memories and in-jokes, and the whole pub was united by the end of the game.

Figure 5.3 The Secrets and Spies end-game.
Credit: Playful Learning Conference by Mark Power.

The game was intended for a group of largely strangers. The brief was to create a game that had low barriers to entry – and that individuals could choose to join in or sit out at any point in the evening. I also wanted to design the entry point (the trailhead or rabbit hole) so that once people had eaten (and drunk) a little, and were more relaxed, they could choose to join in and still have a full experience no matter how far other players had already progressed. In fact, through the social deduction element, the game demanded the teams take on new members; this, alongside the desire to have fresh eyes look at a puzzle that was proving tricky, means these late-comers were brought up to speed quickly. It was to take place in a pub we had sole use of, and this was to provide the backdrop for the game narrative. I also needed a theme that would be immediately self-explanatory to the participants.

The name revealed in the conference programme, Secrets and Spies, immediately communicates both the theme, and the intention. Non-participants could simply look mysterious or disinterested and still be very much 'in-character' as far as the playing participants were concerned. Play or do not play; but of course, a real spy would say that they weren't playing, wouldn't they?

Conference attendees received a simple coded invitation in their conference pack. On arrival, the game immediately began, with several codes the players could crack at once, and both hidden and visible puzzles to find. The bar staff had been briefed to respond to certain code words and passphrases (there was a cheat sheet behind the bar), and the game began in earnest when each player collected their Top Secret envelope with their spy identity and further instructions.

The game was played in three acts, which progress naturally from the game play and deductions made by the players:

1   Entry puzzles and social deduction. The first part of the game is about finding Agency teammates, and this can take some time. This social deduction elongates the game, makes it more about co-operation than competition, and gives people the opportunity to introduce themselves to each other in a playful way. Players find and crack some initial codes to join an Agency, receive an identity and try to find other Agency members while avoiding spies.
2   Puzzle solving, code-cracking and missions. The meat of the game is gathering information, solving puzzles, communicating in code, finding hidden objects. Still avoiding enemy spies and trying to find out what happened to the code-master.
3   It's a trap! Evade and escape. Uncover the double-agents, solve the remaining puzzles and the final conundrum and save the world.

At the start, during the first act, the players were concerned with their own immediate plot line – finding their fellow agency members by using secret messages and code words. In the second act, players started teaming up to solve puzzles and to negotiate with other teams for information they did not yet possess. By the third and final act, they all realised something was very, very wrong, and unless they all worked together to solve the final conundrum, the world would suffer the consequences.

Key to the success of the game were the bar staff, who could introduce new props and tools such as UV torches to reveal messages in UV ink when prompted with the right key phrase. I also co-opted several people to give a nudge where needed throughout the evening, but no one got more than one hint, and they were not allowed to give it to their own team. All of the elements of the game were disguised as part of the fixtures and fittings of the location (or hidden from view to be found or released when the right passphrase is given to the bar staff or handler – the in-character games-master).

The game ended when all the logic puzzle clues had been solved to reveal the super-spy double-agent. Some of the information uncovered was redundant, as it could be surmised from other information, so players did not need to solve every puzzle to deduce the correct outcome only to be certain of it.

It took a lot of work to set up the ciphers and codes, but with a team of helpers, each creating just one of the puzzles, the game was still playable and enjoyable by all, even those who had assisted in the making of part of it. The misspelled menu was a great way to pull people into the game, and with one on every table, it just took one person to notice for everyone at that table to be able to take the bait.

Depending on the group, the game could be played with more role play and disguises. The bar staff or games-masters' table could have any number of additional props, costumes and puzzles to give out in return for codes and passphrases. Players could earn briefcases that unlocked to reveal disguises and instructions for 'secret rendezvous' that made for amusing viewing for spectators and participants alike. I have since created a game that relied almost entirely on just asking the right person (the locked container) the right passcode (the key), and this worked to eliminate the need for physical locked boxes completely. Having more puzzles that could be solved by everybody, for example by doctoring a drinks menu and a children's menu, would allow more participants to work together without having to leave their tables.

More could be made of the helpers taking on roles momentarily to move the action forward, to drop additional puzzles or information in areas already searched; this also gives a chance for the true thespians to reveal themselves. I also think there is an opportunity for players to take on additional optional missions to earn points, scavenger-hunt style. For example, photographing a rival spy being sneaky, or tricking them into saying a passphrase, such as 'bacon and eggs', in a sentence that is being surreptitiously recorded. In this way, it could be expanded to become a full conference game.

The game concluded with the correct unveiling of the super-spy. In practice, few people witnessed this, and the denouement lacked impact. In future, I would aim to either stage something much larger – perhaps with the help of a soundtrack to draw attention – or provide a filmed denouement that could be viewed by any participant with a mobile phone. It could also end with the discovery and unlocking of a final suitcase containing information for the conference, or simply a pile of fun rewards and sweets, or perhaps 'we cracked it' placards for the victory photos.

Conclusion

Some people prefer social activities to get to know fellow delegates, while others prefer to work together on tasks and avoid any form of self-disclosure. These tasks can have a clear win state or just be about creating something together. A task that allows participants to work together for a common outcome will provide an opportunity for participants to introduce themselves. Lengthy introductions can be avoided by using stickers on name badges and making full use of the digital back channel created for an event. Be wary of 'trusted old chestnuts' activities that are now outdated in their expectations for everyone to muck in together and act in the same way. Allowing those who choose to take a different role does not negate an activity. It is better for people to be comfortable than forcibly socialised, especially in a conference where participants may already be out of their comfort zones. Creating opportunities for participants to bond over playful challenges will help remove barriers to learning and playing and create shared memories upon which community and relationships can be built.

Depending on what you want to get from an interlude, dividing activities into icebreakers, group-builders, energisers or parting of ways helps clarify the choice based on what is happening next at an event and what engagement you are hoping for from the participants. An icebreaker simply announces the start of an event with a low-risk activity. A group-builder provides opportunities to create rapport over a shared task, sometimes with an element of competition to allow groups to develop independence from each other. An energiser raises the tempo and renews focus, and is by its nature physical to some degree. A parting of ways activity at the end of the conference should be both a celebration and a reflection. This interlude has a dual role: giving participants the time to step out and reflect on what they have achieved and what they have learnt from what they didn't achieve; and allowing delegates to make last-minute plans to connect with other participants before they leave if they want to carry on their conversations and collaborations when they are back in their 'real' world.

6 Playful Training

Andrew Walsh

Introduction

The techniques I cover here are grounded in social constructivism. The idea that learners build upon prior knowledge and understanding to integrate new facts, knowledge and understanding is central to constructivism. Social constructivism goes further, recognising that the culture and community in which we are situated influences our understanding and that knowledge exists as something that is co-constructed with our community: it does not stand alone (Vygotsky, 1978). Whether training in a workplace or educational setting, it is important to recognise this social constructivist approach to knowledge, as it allows us to use appropriate pedagogical approaches to enable learning to develop to suit the appropriate workplace, subject or professional context.

Play is inherently a social activity, encouraging exploration and creativity within a safe environment. In a training setting, it lets people experiment with new ideas and skills, integrating them into their own experience and prior knowledge and working together with colleagues to develop shared understanding and approaches, the very essence of social constructivism.

Often constructivist and social constructivist approaches to training, whether active learning, enquiry-based learning, problem-based learning or playful learning, can be uncomfortable for learners who are used to more didactic styles of instruction. They may be unsure how to behave and reluctant to engage, wanting instead to be fed facts (that they may struggle to integrate into their existing knowledge) rather than truly learn new things. This chapter will describe ways in which playful approaches can be used that give the learners permission to play in various ways, breaking down the barriers inherent in using training approaches such as play that learners may be unfamiliar or uncomfortable with.

I also mention playfulness and being playful in this chapter. By this, I mean an openness to engaging in play, to having fun, to exploring the opportunities available. Rather than play itself, playfulness is an approach to a situation that enables us to take advantage of opportunities to play, and as such is strongly related to the notion of permission to play. In the words of Bernie De Koven (De Koven, 2014), "playfulness is all about being vulnerable, responsive, yielding to the moment ... You are loose. Responsive. Present." (p. 34).

Permission to Play

People attend training events with preconceived ideas of how they will act and learn during the training. This will be strongly influenced by past experiences and perceived social norms, which can be difficult to shift during the training itself. To become playful during training, they need to give themselves permission to play, they need to feel they have the permission of their workplace and wider social groupings and they need explicit and implicit permission from any trainers too.

Without this 'permission to play' from multiple routes, playful training is likely to be less successful – people may take part in the activities presented but not truly be playing, and so fail to gain the advantages of play. A classic example in training is the use of 'role play', where trainers flag up in advance that this approach will be used, giving attendees explicit permission to play beforehand and usually during the session too, but which instantly pushes many attendees into a less playful mode. They have explicit statements from the trainer giving them permission to play, but their previous experiences may warn them to expect the session to be uncomfortable or embarrassing for them. Deterding (2018) focusses in particular on embarrassment in these situations, using the language of 'alibis' that are needed to play. In this example, the trainer gives only one, fairly weak, alibi to escape that embarrassment, but past experiences, and the social expectations of how participants feel they must act with colleagues, can easily override it.

These ideas come originally from the work of Goffman (1986), who discusses how we see and react to an activity is influenced strongly by the 'frame' in which we see it. Internal and external prompts (keys) and conventions allow a group to define, or fail to define, an activity as play. Goffman discusses play in detail, giving details of nine things that must be sustained to "transform serious, real action into something playful" (p. 41), but in this chapter I will focus on how appropriate keys, prompts or alibis can allow participants to feel that any playful behaviour designed into the activity is appropriate. I will describe how 'embarrassment' (Goffman, 1967), caused by acting differently to the norms of expected behaviour, can be reduced by appropriate keying of the training.

Individual Permission to Play

Although we talk about the individual allowing themselves to play during training, it is not something that is under complete control of that individual; instead, it is something that emerges in relationship to others in the social situation. Extroverted individuals tend to exhibit more playfulness (Lockwood & O'Connor, 2017; Peterson & Seligman, 2004), and it is also related to creativity (Lieberman, 1977), but even the most extroverted and creative individuals are likely to hover on the verge of giving themselves permission to play. Instead, they will tentatively signal (in words and action) to others in the group to see if they feel the same way, and only when others positively return those signals will they feel free to move into a playful frame (Glenn & Knapp, 1987).

The ability to give oneself permission to play is therefore dependent partly on personality and previous experience. However, it is also dependent on how easily participants can signal to each other their willingness to play in any situation. As trainers and creators of playful events, we can build in low-risk opportunities for that signalling to take place between attendees. For example, by the use of playful objects. When running events where groups are sat around tables in a training room, I provide a variety of objects that allow people to signal their willingness to play to one another in a safe, low-risk, way. Bubble mixture, modelling dough, playful sweets (such as popping candy, or whistling lollies) and materials to doodle on (with colourful pens) are all examples of such objects. Anything that people can pick up and easily play with helps signal to other attendees that it is OK to play during the training, without having to state it to one another verbally. They also enable very low-risk play and so can act as a gateway to more involved forms of play led by the trainer.

Anything we can do to break down social barriers between participants can also help them express willingness to play to one another, without which they will tend not to allow themselves permission to play, seeking to avoid embarrassment instead. Icebreakers are a long-established way of doing this (as discussed in Chapter 5), and many are available in books on training techniques, but it is worth looking outside some of this literature towards more explicitly playful ideas, such as the work of Boal (2002), as they embed play directly into the activities themselves.

We must also be aware of privilege and social advantage within the area of personal permissions to play. It is easier for members of some social or racial groupings to expose themselves to possible embarrassment than for others to do the same. Once members of a privileged group have spoken, it is then harder for others to do so, especially if they have an alternate opinion. For instance, women are less likely to ask questions in academic seminars, but only if a man asked a question first (Carter, Croft, Lukas, & Sandstrom, 2018). It is important, therefore, to encourage and enable underrepresented or underprivileged voices to be heard first. For instance, use icebreakers that allow people to interact with small numbers of people at a time, rather than a whole group, or be careful about who is prompted to speak or act first. Make sure that activities and materials are accessible to all who attend so that some are not excluded from the start.

Institutional Permission to Play

Institutional permission to play is difficult to draw out. Even when benefits of play and playful approaches are recognised and valued in institutions, this tends to be focussed on building stronger teams with better communication (Owler, Morrison, & Plester, 2010; Statler, Roos, & Victor, 2009). Play is rarely seen as a normal way of acting within the work environment, so there is an (often correct) assumption that openly playing will be disapproved of by the management structures within that environment.

Attending a playful training event with colleagues from your own or similar workplaces ports across those expectations. In the training event, you are still at work, so the expectations still exist that you *should not play*. Play is transgression against the normal social expectations within the workplace. We should not be frivolous, or choose to have fun, because work is *serious* and in some way we are cheating our workplaces if we play while at work. There is a limited amount of institutional permission embedded within the approval to attend such an event, but I often see this permission being disbelieved by attendees. Social media postings may express surprise they are playing at work, with a tweeter at a recent workshop I ran posting a picture of their activity and stating: 'I'm at work. Honestly'. The permission to attend may, therefore, need reinforcing by more explicit permission to play from an employer.

The simplest way of giving institutional permission to play is to have representation of senior management levels taking part in playful training events. A senior manager actively playing in the session strongly frames the situation as 'allowed' or even 'expected' within the organisation. There are risks of senior management involvement of course, with the possibility of attendees being less open than otherwise in any reflection on themselves or their organisation. A half-way house to this is for a senior manager to explicitly endorse the training approach for attendees, rather than taking part in the actual training event.

Case Study 13: Playful Challenge Cards (Andrew Walsh)

These cards were used in a large team, spread across several offices, as well as in an induction exercise for new students at a UK university. There are two instances of the challenge cards described below, which aimed to achieve slightly different things. The cards used by staff within a workplace were aimed to reduce barriers between different groups of workers, improve communication and improve teamworking. This was through visiting others within their workspaces, carrying out fun and creative exercises and building personal relationships across teams. The cards used by new university students had the additional aim of exploring the physical space of the university and the local area, to improve a sense of 'belonging' and help improve retention statistics.

For the workplace challenge, after some informal awareness raising beforehand, challenge cards were left on staff desks over a weekend for people to discover the following week. There were 104 different challenges, but they were based around a small number of themes. Examples included:

'Give someone from another team a tour of your desk';
'Take a selfie with someone from another team with paper hats on';
'Find someone from another team with a birthday this month and make
    them a birthday card'.

When completed, each challenge could be evidenced by a photo on social media or a comment on the back of the card. New cards were released every month for three months.

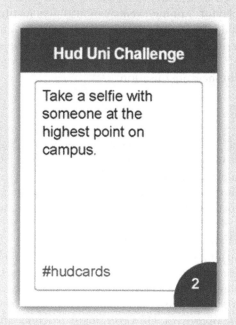

Figure 6.1 Example of a playful challenge card.
Credit: Andrew Walsh.

For the new students, there was an increased focus on exploring the university and local area, and cards were given out on a single occasion for each group of students. The use of the cards with staff was intended to last three months, but it was too hard to maintain the enthusiasm and engagement after the first one or two challenges. It worked much better as a one-day exercise with the students.

We almost had an epic fail with one of the student groups, but it turned into an epic win instead. A group had the challenge of finding the highest point on campus but took the wrong lift and ended up in the university's senior management offices and asked the vice chancellor for a selfie! Luckily, he was happy to play along and loved meeting the students and talking about the challenges they were carrying out.

Any activity that crosses over from a discrete training event to the normal work day would also help to give institutional approval for playful training. Playful challenge cards help to embed a culture of playfulness and acceptance of play as a valid approach within an organisation, in addition to their other benefits. Giving explicit permission, particularly in advance, to apply the knowledge learnt in playful training events can also give institutional validity to the approach and help attendees take full advantage of any event. By this, I mean not just permission to try things within the attendees' personal professional practice, but a willingness for them to try it as an approach for wider groups within their organisation.

Trainer Permission to Play

This is the area where the trainer can make the most difference. You can give small nudges that facilitate institutional permission to play, you can feed into personal permission to play, but this section details some ways in which you can explicitly and implicitly encourage play. Some approaches to creating a context in which play is clearly allowed and encouraged are covered, but these examples are obviously not exhaustive.

Before covering individual activities, we should consider learning objectives and how to use them. Learning objectives are incredibly important, enabling us to have a clear idea of the outcomes we hope attendees to achieve as a result of any training. With clear, concise, well-constructed learning objectives, we can plan the training in a way that gives everyone an opportunity to meet those objectives. However, many teaching and training books will go on to say that we should discuss these in detail with attendees of any training. Displaying them during the training would be widely seen as best practice. In the context of playful training, and indeed much training where the tutor interacts fully with their audience, this is not true.

One of the benefits of play is that it allows the players to change the rules as they go along. To paraphrase De Koven (2014), games change the players to suit the game, play changes the rules to suit the players, or in this case, we could say that playful training changes the outcomes to suit the players.

Learning Outcomes

The details of activities and discussions we use should vary depending on the context of any particular training session, with the prior knowledge and context of the attendees valued enough for it to trump any prior detailed learning objectives. Playful training trusts any attendees to know what they most need to learn, allowing it to be truly useful and potentially transformational in a way that sticking to firm learning objectives would not be. If we have planned the session well, attendees will be equipped to meet our learning objectives anyway, even if that occurs outside the session. If we display, or too explicitly refer to, detailed learning objectives, then this can lock attendees into focussing on these at the expense of more useful and transformational learning that may otherwise take place. Incidentally, this is precisely why we are normally encouraged to display learning outcomes, as it is normally seen as good practice to restrict learning to those outcomes we have previously identified as important. Playful training should recognise that allowing learning outcomes to change according to the needs of participants is one of the features that makes it particularly powerful, rather than a flaw that needs preventing.

Case Study 14: SEEK! The Search Skills Game (Andrew Walsh)

This game is used in teaching search skills to adult learners within further and higher education. It aims to bring discussion and active learning to a 20-minute segment of a research or library skills session.

SEEK! is a simple card game for up to eight players, taking roughly ten minutes to play, which has been used regularly (with updates) since 2012, including in class sizes of up to 60 students, with multiple games running at the same time. It includes questions on: extracting keywords from assignment titles; advanced search tips; the information cycle; synonyms and alternative terms; and wildcards.

Some of the questions have no 'right' answer, often requiring the group to decide if an answer is satisfactory. The game allows players to get similar questions repeatedly wrong or right in a low-risk environment, as well as having their prior knowledge gently challenged by some of the questions. It is then followed by a ten-minute whole-class discussion phase that raises issues covered by questions in the game. The facilitator's instructions suggest topics and questions to cover in this discussion in order to draw out learning points and deepen understanding.

Although there are set rules included within the game, I never force people to stick to them absolutely and often allow them to play with the cards in different ways. The cards are also colour-coded by category of questions, allowing it to be easily varied across classes by removing one of the colours of cards.

Figure 6.2 Example of a SEEK! challenge card.
Credit: Andrew Walsh.

Simple Non-Digital Games

An easy way of bringing play into training is through the use of simple, non-digital card or board games. To improve the information skills of students, I often use simple games like Seek!, or card-based referencing games (see Case Study 3). I make sure these games are short and easily adaptable, using them to replace alternative active learning exercises in a session rather than them taking up the whole of any particular training event.

As we are discussing *play* rather than specifically *games* in training, it is worth pointing out that play and games can be slightly different things.

Educational games can have limited amounts of 'free' or 'imaginative' play within them (what Caillois & Barash, 2001 called *paida*) and large amounts of fairly restrictive, rule-based play (*ludus*).

Much of what we think of as play, along with the benefits discussed elsewhere, belong to the paidic end of that spectrum, though the rules that go along with card and board games tend to sit towards the ludic end. So, to prevent these games becoming no more than simple active learning exercises, I enable and encourage the players to adapt the rules if they wish, to prevent them being limited by the ludic nature of a simple card or board game. These card *games* therefore can become a route for increasing the amount of *play* in my training.

Layout of the Room and Use of Space

The training space you use, and the layout of it, sets social expectations within your learners. If it is laid out as rows of chairs facing the front, you set the expectation, the frame (Goffman, 1986), that there will be an expert stood at the front, feeding the 'audience' information. Those are the social cues you are choosing to push onto attendees of a training event by accepting such a layout.

Instead, change the layout and your use of space to frame it as playful, or at the very least, collaborative. Resist the urge to be at the front, stood behind a lectern, lecturing. Lay out rooms so (as a minimum) people are sat in groups and you can move amongst them, helping to equalise the perceived power dynamics between trainer and trainee. If you do not need to be sat in a room, then consider activities and discussions while people are walking (try a timed learning walk, with your group split into pairs) or using the space in any way that does not reinforce those expectations of passive learning but instead encourages play.

You can also disrupt the expectations present in large groups based in lecture theatres through activities that split them temporarily into smaller groups (see also Chapter 11). There are classic examples of this such as 'buzz groups', where the whole lecture theatre is split into groups of two or three people for discussions, but there are other ways of enabling this split too. As a small variation on this, it can be useful to ask alternate rows of people to turn around and work in small groups with the people behind them, which disrupts the sense that they must look forward towards the 'expert' at the front of the room. Group identity can be focussed along natural breaks in a lecture theatre, such as using walkways to form teams in playful activities – this can work well for interactive quizzes to set up a playful rivalry across the room. Rows within lecture theatres can form smaller groups, though it can be difficult for people to work together in such a constrained linear format. It does suit playful activities where several tasks need doing in sequence though, progressing as an activity passes down the row!

An example of this type of activity is Lecture Theatre Writing & Citing, a little activity based around keeping track of sources of information and citing properly as you go. Prepare in advance a set of cards or sheets of papers with extracts of information on them. These could be extracts from book chapters or journal articles on the subject matter being covered, or generic materials if you wish (facts about penguins, perhaps?). Each card or sheet of paper should have enough information on it to create a proper reference. For the activity, drop a set of these information cards at the end of each row of a lecture theatre, together with a blank sheet of A4 paper. Tell your students to write a sentence on the blank sheet, in their own words, based on a fact from one of the information cards. They then mix up the pack of information cards and pass everything to the next person along. Give a short amount of time (around ten minutes, depending on the length of your lecture theatre rows), for it to make it to the end of each row. Once the time is up, give the final person in each row an extra task. They must work out which information card was used for each sentence. This illustrates how time-consuming it can be matching up sources with your work unless you do it as you are writing!

Disruption of Training Dynamics

Linked to the use of space, there are other activities you can use to disrupt the normal expectations of learning and encourage a shift in frame. These can be carried out even within environments like lecture theatres that will tend to discourage a playful mindset. A simple, classic example is the use of an object that symbolises interaction in some way. So throwing a beach ball around a lecture theatre, with each person who catches the ball expected to make a contribution of some sort to a room-wide discussion. Soft, throwable wireless microphones are the modern version of this.

Case Study 15: Pass the Parcel (Katie Piatt)

A pass the parcel game was designed to be a conference icebreaker during an opening plenary session for the 2016 Playful Learning Conference, as part of the Marbles and Missions conference game (see Case Study 25). Pass the Parcel, as a game that many delegates are likely to have been familiar with from their childhoods, aimed to recreate the emotions of play: fear (that it might land on you and you get a challenge) and excitement (that you might get a prize). The activity also aimed to encourage delegates to get to know each other through the forfeits.

Before the event, nine identical parcels were made, each with a 'special' marble in the centre as a prize, with six other layers in different colours each containing a slip of paper with a challenge and two 'normal' marbles. A parcel was sent out to each row of seats in the lecture theatre, and then the music began. The parcels were then passed backwards and forwards along each row. When the music stopped, the person holding the parcel unwrapped one layer had to complete the challenge using the marbles. Challenges required the player to interact with other delegates, for example:

"Exchange marbles with the person in your row who looks most like you."
"Give your marbles to the person in the row in front of you."

Using one parcel per row worked well and made use of the lecture theatre arrangement. The challenges provided humour and interaction without putting people too far out of their comfort zones. The whole activity took around ten minutes, as no further discussion was required. Depending on the theme of an event or backgrounds of an audience, the contents of the parcels and challenges can be adapted to suit.

Activities that prompt social memories of play when younger can be particularly useful to disrupt expectations from passive and didactic to interactive and social. A children's game like pass the parcel brings with it shared childhood memories of play for many people, as well as disrupting the use of space and communication in a playful way.

Use of Construction and Metaphor in Training

Building tools such as LEGO can help us use metaphor effectively within a playful training situation. The best-known example of using building tools is LEGO Serious Play™ (see Case Study 36), but these approaches can be taken using other tools and with slightly different approaches (see Case Study 34). In these approaches, we ask trainees to construct or draw something that acts as a metaphor for the subject we want them to discuss. The tools, whether LEGO, building blocks, modelling clay, pens and paper or anything else you want to use for this approach, invite them to be playful.

Instead of thinking purely within their own heads, participants are encouraged to think (and build with) their hands, an idea I normally refer to as 'embodied cognition' (see Noland & Penny, 2014). It recognises that often we may struggle to make sense of an idea, or to solve a problem, when presented with it in an abstract or purely intellectual way. When we can physically handle objects, manipulating them as we think, this can often help us think through things in a different way. It recognises that we think with our bodies (especially our hands) as well as our minds.

In addition to taking advantage of the idea of embodied cognition, this approach draws on ideas of narrative and storytelling, asking learners not to explain themselves, but in effect to tell a story about their models. Their models become metaphors for the ideas they need to explain, safe to talk about and through, making it a safer, more playful way of expressing ideas than to talk through the same things directly.

I often use LEGO because I feel it helps to remove a perceived need for artistic skill that participants may feel when asked to do a similar exercise with pens and paper. Drawing can make people like myself (who have zero artistic ability) feel exposed, in a way that sticking plastic bricks together does not. It helps to make a clear distinction between building models as a *creative* exercise and building them as an *artistic* one. Whatever the tool used, however, I tend to take the same overall approach. Participants will get the chance to do one or more warm-up exercises to get used to the tool, I will then introduce the idea of building metaphors, before carrying out the main exercise(s) in earnest.

There will be a small number of rules that everyone must agree on, including most importantly that whatever the creator of a model says it is, that's what it is ('If I say my Play-Doh sausage represents the ineffable vastness of creation, then it does ...'). I will take care to always ask participants about their models (not ask them the question again that inspired the model), so reinforcing that they can talk at arm's length about their thoughts in a safe way. I will also try not to interpret the models myself, but allow and encourage their creator to do so, asking questions that may draw out that information.

Creative Production

There are links between creativity and play, with the creative approaches mentioned here clearly representing a type of play. The approaches do not depend on any level of artistic ability however, and are carefully selected to ensure that they represent *creative* approaches, accessible to most people, not *artistic* ones, that exclude those without those artistic abilities.

One creative production method that is particularly effective is using scissors and glue to re-arrange sources of information. Where we might have articles, news stories, book chapters or any other information sources capable of being printed, this approach helps to break down the sense that the knowledge is somehow sacrosanct, or beyond the ability of our learners to both access and manipulate. One approach I take is to give journal articles to students and ask them to cut up that article and re-arrange the content in ways that make it more accessible to them. This might be to pull out key phrases and sentences that allow them to critique the article (I normally give them a structure to follow for this, e.g. methodology representing the foundations of a house, reason for writing the article = the walls, etc.). It might be to help them summarise an article (glue key points onto the front of a piece of card, along with bibliographic details on the back), or even just to help them sum up and remember what the information might be useful for (cut out words and phrases to build a "found poem" that shows why it might be useful (or not) in future). Whatever the exact purpose or way of doing it, this approach gives them permission to interact and play with a text that might otherwise be inaccessible to them and encourages them to play with such texts in future.

Polling and Quizzes

This approach can be the gateway drug of playful training, allowing trainers to gently move from a more traditional approach to one that directly encourages play. Whether asking questions of participants in a low-technology way (e.g. hold up pieces of card, stand up/sit down, etc.), or something using polling or quiz software, you can gain the same playful benefits in a way that can be low-risk for the trainer as well as the learners.

Use this approach to allow learners to answer questions in a fun way, perhaps bringing in elements of competition that can encourage some learners. It shows participants that they are allowed to contribute, to "have their voice heard", without exposing themselves as individuals. This playful encouragement to answer questions can help them see value in their own knowledge and opinions as the training continues, encouraging further interaction in the session.

Escape Rooms

A playful training approach I take that perhaps most clearly gives participants permission to play is that of using an escape room-style approach (see Case Study 23). Although I never have a dedicated room for learners to escape from, I use the idea of 'an escape room in a box', which provides many of the same benefits. In a standard escape room, players become immersed in the game through a combination of the physical space (a locked room or series of rooms), the narrative that runs through the game and the challenge of getting to the end of a series of puzzles. A portable escape room does much the same, except the physical space is reduced to a box (or series of boxes) in a restricted space. I find that a table containing all the materials for an escape room activity acts quite effectively as a *magic circle* that helps participants transition from the normal world into the playful one.

This demarcation between the normal training environment and one in which they are playing an escape room game acts effectively to signal permission to play. The boxes and associated puzzles, the narratives that normally sit alongside them, the challenge of 'winning' against the escape room, all signal that play is not only OK, but expected and rewarded.

Alongside this, the team-based nature of completing escape rooms recognises the different levels of willingness and ability to play likely to be present in any group of learners, especially if we manage to build a range of puzzle types into an educational escape room-style activity. It is fine for someone reluctant to play to stand back slightly and point out things that others may have missed, just as it is fine for another participant to enthusiastically throw themselves at every puzzle. As an activity, it helps enable different levels of willingness to play as long as participants contribute something towards the team's challenges.

Conclusion

Playful training, here seen as essentially a social constructivist approach, can help us run training events that enable contextually-appropriate learning to take place. It can only work, however, if we can help learners break away from the 'anti-play' expectations of many educational and workplace settings. If we do not address the idea that participants need permission to play, then we may struggle to make this approach effective. This permission can come from themselves, especially if it can help them to break down social barriers and signal that play is 'OK' to each other. The permission can come from their institutions, especially if senior managers are seen being playful, or if activities leak into everyday work-life. Most importantly as trainers, however, is how we signal permission to play to our learners, through techniques such as flexible learning outcomes; small games; disrupting expectations of space and dynamics; the use of metaphor; creative activities; quizzes; or specific game type approaches such as escape rooms.

Although as trainers we have the most direct influence on how we give participants permission to play, to be most effective we need to bear in mind the permission the learners need to give themselves, and the pressure institutional permission – or lack of permission – may put on, which may reduce their ability to engage fully in playful learning. All three areas must be borne in mind when designing playful training to enable us to be successful across the different settings in which we may work.

7 Running a Playful Event

Emily Shields

Introduction

Managing playfulness, or playful people, during an event can be a challenge. Dimming enthusiasm, suspending a 'sense of disbelief' or breaking the game's 'magic circle' could quite easily ruin a delegate's experience of the event or – in extreme cases – the event itself. However, there are times when information needs to be given, decisions need to be made and speakers have to present; not in itself a non-playful experience, but one that needs to be controlled by the speaker. Managing these practicalities sometimes requires a non-playful, purely practical approach that needs to be handled carefully in order not to disturb the overall sense of playfulness.

The ethos of playfulness can also be used during the planning process: a good way to ensure that the event itself is infused with a playful attitude. Managing such preparations through a conference team or committee requires a level of practicality while allowing team members to immerse themselves within a playful environment. Creating a game-like space within which ideas can be fostered and just as often discarded is an important part of the planning process. Understanding how to create a 'magic circle', a place where certain game rules are accepted by the players (Huizinga, 1955) in which playfulness and practicalities form the rule-set, is crucial to an effective planning process.

All events will have boundaries and constraints that are beyond your control: the physical environment, the number of delegates, organisational expectations and budgets. However, as Bogost (2016) states, this is not necessarily a bad thing, as too much choice can hinder a playful attitude as much as too little. Having boundaries set for us to work within gives the planning team a defined space in which to play. He also suggests that *everything* can be treated as play, and while this approach may be difficult to apply for those setting out on this process and facing the organisational behemoth of planning and organising an event, it is an admirable aim.

The benefit of being playful in both planning and implementation is that no one can predict what will unfold, and the learning and development goals that can be attained are unlimited. A playful event sets parameters, gives a space in which normal rules are mutable and lets the players take themselves on unexpected journeys. As organisers, this can be a challenge to manage while keeping the event running as planned, as I will discuss later in this chapter.

Case Study 16: Social Media All-Stars Card Game (Liz Cable)

This card game was created for a conference involving coached cohorts of small business owners. It aimed to teach the principles of social media in a way that would provoke discussion and swapping of personal experiences and was designed to reward prioritising time taken for training, strategy and review over action.

The aim of the game is to get the most Sales, which was made easier by growing your online Influence. It assumes each business owner can spare 60 minutes over the course of each week to deal with social media, which equates to taking one Action card, or two of any other cards (Strategy, Training and Review) each turn. These cards then affect Sales and Influence. If Influence is awarded, then dice are rolled to increase influence, representing *liking*, *sharing*, *following* and *viral* – to show the somewhat random nature of social media. The advice on the cards was subsequently written up as an action plan and widely circulated.

The trainees really liked the STAR (Strategy, Training, Action, Review) model, and the advice on the cards, but the mechanics of the game did not work as it was played on the day, although it did spark the discussion around Influence and its effect on Sales, which was the original intent. A last-minute request to let the coaches have a 'special role' in their business support group meant instead of playing along, they were choosing each turn how many dice of their own to roll to add to each player's roll depending on how good they thought the idea was, which imbalanced the game mechanics. The lesson is to never change the rules without playtesting the consequences first.

Pre-Event Planning

No matter how large the event planning team is, the same principles should apply. As with every successful team, it is good to have a range of people and skills, which would mean that not every committee member will be brimming with ideas of playful activity; indeed, someone with a constructively critical attitude can be a bonus to any team. Ideas are needed, but someone with the pragmatic skills to make those ideas a reality is also necessary, and this is not always the same person. In terms of practical skills for a successful planning team, it is useful to have those with skillsets including event management, financial acumen, design skills; and for a large event, it will be important to get on board a representative from the venue to advise you (for more information on organisational planning, see Chapter 3).

Alongside any skillset individual members bring, what all team members also need is to embrace a playful attitude; if the team members do not value it, then the likelihood of delegates engaging at the event is reduced. However, you are not always in a position to choose the people who you will be organising the event with, and it may be an uphill battle to get the wider team to encompass a playful ethos. Getting committee members on board with your ideas to create a playful event (or to integrate playful elements to an existing event) is an important step and the first one to tackle at the pre-planning stage. It may be that you need to make a case for playfulness and to coach your team members in the ethos. An understanding of how the committee, as well as delegates at the event, can benefit from a more creative and less constrained approach will be an important scene-setter early on.

Some conferences, like Playful Learning and Counterplay, are specific in that play is at the very heart of what they do, and the planning team and delegates are like-minded individuals who need no introduction to the power of play. However, most events are not quite so play-centric, and it is useful to decide at an early stage what level of playfulness you are aiming for. The fully-integrated playful conference is at one end of the spectrum, while most other events will have elements of playfulness combined with a more traditional approach. The planning for these latter events may differ slightly, with a 'playful' team member charged with running particular aspects in an otherwise traditional event.

Making the planning process more playful and encouraging a playful attitude among the committee can take a number of small steps:

- Play a game at the start to free up ideas and get into a playful state of mind. An 'icebreaker' activity is a good way to get the team playing, having fun and getting to know each other: see Case Studies 10 and 17 for examples.
- Try to make mundane aspects of the meeting fun. Offer chocolate rewards to those who take on actions; ask attendees to bring along something that represents their attitude to play to get the ball rolling; bring dice along to randomise the agenda; have at least one agenda item that is creative and encourages discussion.
- Get ideas on paper. You are more likely to find a good idea in the midst of 30 ideas than in one or two. Rapid idea generation is a tool used in many creative design approaches: a playful version could include

something like 'six-eight-five', where people are given five minutes and eight post-its to list six to eight ideas. Sharing and discussing these in turns leads to far-reaching yet useful ideas. Even the silliest ideas can turn out to have practical applications: a pirate-themed treasure map can turn into a playful venue map.

At the planning stage, it is important to understand who your delegates are, and their likely objectives, in order to create playful experiences that they are more likely to engage in (see Chapter 4). Exploring why you are employing playful approaches and what your attendees will achieve from this is important in ensuring that you understand what it is you are offering. Do you want activities that will enhance the event and are entwined throughout (see Chapter 10), or are you looking for activities that will sit separately and run parallel to it? Can you be flexible enough to allow your delegates to define the playfulness levels if you are unsure of how immersed they will be in the process (see Case Study 8)? No matter how big your event, there will be times when you also need to interface with more formal elements of

Figure 7.1 Catering staff getting in the pirate mood at Playful Learning 2018.
Credit: Nicola Whitton.

an organisation or environment: estates, finance departments, HR, catering and those whose everyday working space is being entered. Often playfulness can be embraced by willing participants, such as the Playful Learning catering staff who were willing to dress as pirates; or delegates from another conference joining in open activities or social media games. However, this is not always the case, and you will need to be mindful of the needs of others outside of the event but sharing the space or online platform.

The pre-event planning should also include discussion on how best to 'warm up' your delegates. Not everyone will happily throw themselves into a playful situation if they do not know to expect it. While you do not need to detail the exact activities that will be happening, if you want your delegates to be open to games and play, then you need to plan ahead for this and set the tone accordingly. As Sicart (2014) suggests, if you want individuals to know that this particular context is a context for play, then you need to embed cues and signal that your event is open to playfulness. You can embed such cues throughout the planning process. For instance, if your correspondence is fairly serious and academic, then there will be a disconnect on arrival if you present people with an obvious playful environment. You can indicate early on that play is encouraged by utilising official channels such as emails, the call for papers and the website to embed playfulness before arrival. If you are planning activities that require some preparation by your delegates, be clear about this and send out information beforehand. People can always choose to opt out, but not being able to engage because you had not brought the right tools or known what to expect can act as a form of exclusion.

At this stage, a decision should be made regarding how play will integrate into your event as there are options for all levels of playfulness. Are you looking to create an entirely playful event with an over-arching game (see Chapter 10) or a theme that is complemented throughout with optional games, play and activities for attendees to engage in? Will the games consist of a series of smaller, stand-alone events that still instil an ethos of playfulness but are less time-intensive for the organisers to prepare? Individual games like this could be run throughout the event, or alternatively, you could pick times that would work within your programme, such as an evening event or over a lunch break. If you do not feel ready to plan and run an event-specific game, you could encourage free-play where the delegates themselves create the play. Utilising creative elements such as LEGO, Plasticine, art materials, dice, etc., organisers can foster delegates' playfulness. Beware though, this is not the easy option! While the materials may be available, the environment and context still need to say 'play' in order for your attendees to have the attitude you want to encourage and setting those cues about the environment you want to create needs careful planning. Also bear in mind that if there's incongruence between the event's formal sessions and the planned activities, you may find less playful engagement than you anticipated.

Top tips at the planning stage:

1 Create a safe, playful space for the event committee: where all ideas are valued.
2 Engage with your event-planning colleagues and any related staff (security, catering, tech, volunteers, etc.) early in the process, and share the playful ethos with them (e.g. value their ideas too).
3 Understand the delegates and their expectations and likely engagement with play.
4 Know what you want to achieve and how integrated play will be in the overall event.
5 Plan to set the tone early on and let your delegates, presenters and exhibitors know in advance if there are activities that they may want to engage in or prepare for.
6 Test any games you want to play at the event itself.

When is Play Not Appropriate?

A playful environment is not suitable for every event. While formal academic or industry events should not automatically exclude play, there may well be some research topics where playfulness embedded or even running parallel to the subject matter would not feel acceptable. Likewise, even in the most playful event, there are still important activities and outcomes at the core of the event. As organisers, it would be disrespectful to run noisy, disruptive games alongside sessions where presenters are trying to promote thinking, reflection or to keep the attention of their audience. In all of these situations, playfulness might offer cues for the way the event is run (such as creating a safe space, open idea forums, embracing failure, etc.), rather than overt games.

There may be occasions during the event where you intersect with others using the same space: interactions that also need respecting. If you are using academic or business premises, you are usually in a mixed working environment, and while most people are accepting of some levels of disruption in such large shared spaces, taking this too far may incur the frustrations and potential complaints of those around you. Having to bring games and play to a close prematurely due to the annoyance of those around is a quick way to dissipate any playful environment you may have fostered. On the other hand, engaging positively with those not directly involved in the game can bring extra elements and encourage play amongst more reluctant non-playing delegates. Counterplay takes place in a public library, and many of the workshops or playful objects are available for the general public to access: play there is an open invitation.

There are other times when trying to engage with Bogost's (2016) view that 'everything' can be made playful may well end up in a swift termination of your event booking. Organising a conga to evacuate in the event of a fire alarm would never be a good idea. Being playful around anything concerning budgets and finances is also not to be encouraged.

Case Study 17: Curate-A-Fact (Alex Moseley)

This card-based collaborative game was used as a quick networking activity with around 50 people during the first coffee break at a museums symposium in Belfast. The brief was to run a game to fit into 15 minutes over a coffee break that would introduce people to each other and get them thinking creatively.

Cards were created to represent 50 museum artefacts, using open-source images from museum collections (e.g. Science Museum, British Museum) and each card colour-coded in one of five colours. Attendees were each given a card at registration. After collecting their coffee, they were asked to join together with four or five other people to curate a small themed exhibition using their combined artefacts. None of the cards could be of the same colour, to avoid easy connections (e.g. two Roman artefacts, or two lamps).

After ten minutes, each group was asked to pitch their exhibition to everyone else in 30 seconds. Once all groups had presented their ideas, everyone used their card as a voting chip and placed it next to the group whose idea they most liked. The winning group was the one with the most votes.

The activity worked extremely well, resulting in some very creative ideas. The same activity was then used at a major museums conference in London, with 200 attendees. This time, teams were formed over lunch and were given posters on which to stick their cards and describe their collection: these formed a gallery, and everyone received a sticker to vote on their favourite idea.

Figure 7.2 Curate-A-Fact cards.
Credit: Alex Moseley.

The Playful Event

The planning stage is crucial in ensuring that the right playful environment can be created at the event itself. Underpinning any playful 'chaos' should be a well-managed environment. This environment can be flexible, both in terms of the space itself or the ethos, allowing delegates to build upon any activities you have planned, but the foundations of the playful activities, and the tools to enable these, should already be in place for delegates to engage with.

At the event itself, everyone – committee members, helpers, delegates and sponsors or exhibitors – should know what to expect; expectations that should have been established in pre-event communications. However, there will always be things that do not quite go as predicted, and during your pre-conference preparation you will have thought through many such 'what ifs ...'. When planning for the unexpected, bear in mind that the issues listed below are not particularly uncommon: most of these situations are likely to happen at some point during your playful event career. It is the unique, specific and truly random that can make for difficult situations.

Setting the tone at the event is just as important as managing expectations with pre-event communications. First impressions count, and encouraging attendees to enter the game space/playful environment from the outset encourages subsequent behaviours from your delegates. If it is an event where attendees have to register, a positive registration experience will be key to first interactions and, if you have control over your environment, the space that attendees walk into can also be used creatively. As Sicart (2014) suggests, "good playgrounds open themselves up to play, and their props serve as instruments for playful occupations" (p. 55); playgrounds are not limited to children, but creating a play space for your attendees with playful props, signage, costumes and attitude can inspire play in even the most hesitant delegate.

Registration at an event is the place where your delegates should be feeling excited, refreshed and ready to engage with the event ahead of them. It is the perfect opportunity to set the tone and encourage a playful attitude. Covering the basics is important here, and you should ensure the registration desk is staffed by kindred souls who are fully committed to the playful ethos you are creating. The registration area is the focus for most delegate questions throughout any event, and having well-briefed helpers, enthusiastic about the activities planned, is vital in order to encourage delegates to enthuse in turn. As a focus, the registration area can be a station for the more static fun that you may be trying to encourage, perhaps a creative table for delegates to take some time out from the more formal learning. It is worth noting though that having a table with colouring and creative 'bits and bobs' on it does not in itself make an event playful, but such a table can add to a wider playful atmosphere.

Unprepared Delegates

If you have an activity that requires some preparation on behalf of the delegate, offer time, props or support at the conference itself to allow them to join the game later. For example, having a masked ball as the conference dinner is fine, but it would be wise to have some spare masks. Playful Learning 2017 proposed that delegates' toys could have their own parallel conference, where delegates brought toys along that acted as alter-egos both online and at the conference itself (Jones & Shields, 2018). Many attendees embraced this and brought toys along with them, but those who came without toys could choose their own from a selection the organisers had purchased from a charity shop (see Case Study 11).

Non-Engagement (Individual)

As a playful organiser, it can be hard to accept, but non-engagement shouldn't be perceived as a negative unless a delegate feels excluded through organisational issues rather than their own decision. Carse (1986) noted that "whoever must play, cannot play" (p. 4): play cannot be forced, and so every activity should have a get-out, and one that doesn't make it difficult for someone to say 'no'. If you are trying an activity that requires all delegates at an event to engage, you need to ensure you have an opt-out clause that doesn't mean delegates are missing out on any of the event's main learning objectives. Not every activity will suit every delegate, and even the most playful among us have games we do not want to join in with. Not joining in with the activity itself does not mean someone is not enjoying it or getting something out of it.

Organisers need to ensure that non-engagement is not the result of bad planning on their part. If you have planned a multi-day event where attendees may come on one day only, you need to consider how the individuals attending on days two, three, etc. will join in what could be a well-established game space. Exclusion from a game is different to choosing not to engage, and ensuring that you prepare those joining a game later than others ensures that they can gain frustration-free entry into the game. Planning an approach in advance for day or late delegates is therefore vital.

Non-Engagement (Cohort)

Regardless of how permeated by playful activities the event is, when there is little engagement, this can be harder to deal with at the time and will need careful consideration at the post-event debrief. It may be that there has been a disconnect between the planners' assumptions of their delegates' playfulness and the actuality, or that the activities themselves just were not quite right or had been inadequately explained. Whatever the reasons, this is where the pre-event planning and the ability to be flexible come into their own, as well as a little gentle persuasion from the organisers. If things are not working as you expect, you could try some insider tactics, enlisting the event helpers as well as delegates known to the organisers, to be more proactive in playing and to encourage those around them. If there is a competitive element to the games, strategically planned encouragement of a team ethos can be useful. At events where items (e.g. stars, stickers, coins) are collected to establish a winner, organisers may start handing these out more freely to get the ball rolling or to encourage a closer competition.

Over-Engagement

While playful design may permeate the event's content, at the opposite end of the spectrum you may find over-engagement with play problematic. All events have a timetable, the flexibility of which should be known to the organisers; however, over-engagement of delegates may cause some games to take too long and impact upon the timings for the rest of the conference. The Counterplay conference in 2018 arranged for a band to be part of one morning's activities. The delegates were enjoying this so much that the organisers changed the timetable for the day to allow an extended concert/dance. This level of flexibility is more likely to be possible in a playful environment, and one where the organisers and other presenters are fully aware of the potential for this to happen and the delegates are also happy to respond so positively to an unexpected turn of events. In an event where play is taking longer than expected, gauging the delegate response to cutting short play may be harder to judge, but most attendees are there to engage primarily with content even if they are engaging in play, and managing the need for both is usually accepted.

As with any activity and group of people, you might find that particular individuals or small groups are beginning to spoil the event experience for others (either in or outside of the event). It is a good idea to have an organiser or helper who is looking out for this and is able to reign in the antisocial activity in an appropriate way (maybe by using the game parameters to restrict or refocus activity) to guard against this. If that fails to work, the early engagement with security staff (as discussed above) will ensure you can work with them to solve the problem appropriately.

Case Study 18: Mapping A Story (Liz Cable)

Mapping A Story was created as part of a course on creative writing for the web. ActionBound is an online tool to build location-based games (like scavenger hunts), which can then be played on mobile phones. It allows players to submit different types of media in response to questions: text, photos, audio and answers to multiple-choice questions. There is a free version as well as an educational license.

The game was designed partly as a group-building exercise, to familiarise players with the location of the event and partly to introduce different styles of location-based narratives and practice collaborative writing using digital tools. Many of the players did not know each other, and the teams were put together randomly. No prizes were offered, and the time limit of 45 minutes was simply to get the groups back together at the end to present and share what they had created rather than being integral to the design of the game.

Mapping A Story was very simple, consisting of around ten tasks. After a short introduction, players were sent off in teams of four or five to complete these. The tasks included orientation questions but also introduced a few key concepts and began the process of getting the teams to collaborate on creative work. For example, one challenge asked for an interpretation of a creative brief: take three pictures depicting friendship, perseverance and courage. There was also a short psychogeography walk based on random encounters and a re-interpretation of how to give directions, ending with an instruction to walk to the nearest window and write a haiku about what the group saw.

There were no right or wrong responses to the creative tasks. Experimentation and creative interpretation were encouraged and rewarded in discussion. Even if groups felt they had failed on a task, the presentation at the end demonstrated and celebrated the wildly different responses. The groups had each written their haiku about a different view from a different window. There was no failure, only different interpretations.

Conclusion

There are many ways to infuse an event with playfulness. Options ranging from a full-blown, multi-day conference with a theme and structured game throughout, through to an afternoon event with a few playful interludes and a table of LEGO, means that there are choices available for all organisers. Play can enhance any event if planned in a considered way; successful playful events do not usually just happen, they are carefully orchestrated behind the scenes to give an environment and structure in which everyone can choose to play, spectate or create.

Careful orchestration starts with the planning: without this, all aspects of an event are more likely to fail. Play can look unstructured or even disordered, but behind any event activity is hours' worth of organisation and testing so that the execution can go smoothly and any issues can be dealt with quickly and effectively. To enable this, planning needs to consider and include all parties involved in the event – from the delegates to the catering staff – and all stages and activities from pre-arrival through to the event end.

If this planning is conducted playfully, it can also bring an openness, inclusiveness and creative aspect to the event design. A playful committee is more likely to produce new creative ideas and solutions to many of the common event activities, problems and issues, creating a better experience overall for the delegates.

Finally, remember to expect the unexpected. The beauty of play is that you do not always know where it is going to take you. As organisers, deviation from the plan can be stressful, but if you have prepared what you can and you have thought through contingency strategies, then the rest should take care of itself. If you get really stuck, then play is always there to help you think of creative solutions to any organisational problems that may arise.

Part IV
Engaging People Playfully

8 Creating Immersive Experiences

Giskin Day

Introduction

We traditionally associate the word 'immersion' with being submerged in water, especially in baptism or ritual cleansing. Games that use immersive experiences also aspire to bring about transformation: by being plunged into an alternative reality, players experience the world – and themselves – in different ways, both physically and mentally. Immersive games may curate the environment in a way that places players in situations that are redolent with possibilities for play, like escape rooms (discussed in Chapter 9). Alternatively, these games may cast the players in roles that call for them to negotiate public spaces in new ways, by playing in-character or being called on to act out-of-character at various points in the game.

As 3D technology grows in sophistication and decreases in cost, virtual reality (VR) is growing in popularity as a way of creating immersive experiences for players. Riva and colleagues (2007) showed that a feeling of 'presence' was able to elicit emotional responses, adding to the immersive effects of VR. While VR holds considerable promise for immersive experiences, its current reliance on headsets limits both freedom of movement and the potential for physical, as opposed to virtual, interactions with others. Those of us who enjoy the lo-fi appeal of people, props and place have yet to be convinced that VR can improve on the experience of dynamic, phenomenological play in the real world.

Huizinga (1955) described the frame that circumscribes a game in time and space as 'the magic circle'. The term is appropriate, argue Salen and Zimmerman (2004), because something genuinely magical happens: "a new reality is created, defined by the rules of the game and inhabited by its players" (p. 94–5). Immersion through a new reality can be categorised into three non-exclusive types:

- Immersion as *presence* (after Turner & Turner, 2006), which is the feeling of actually 'being there' in an alternate environment, virtual or real-world.

- Immersion as *absorption* (after Calleja, 2011), which is the sense of deep emotional investment found through uncovering a story or journeying with a character.
- Immersion as *flow* (after Csikszentmihalyi, 1992), which is the sense of being so deeply involved in an appropriately-challenging activity that one loses all sense of time and place.

A successful immersive game may engage the player using all three strategies.

The Mission

In this chapter, I will be drawing on the game 'The Mission', which I developed as a team-building activity, and is provided as an example of an immersive game that does just that. The game can best be described as a hybrid between a LARP (live action role playing) and an ARG (alternate reality game).

Case Study 19: The Mission (Giskin Day)

The Mission was a three-hour away-day game for 50 participants from the Faculty of Education Office in Imperial College's School of Medicine. It aimed to develop team-building through bringing players together who usually work at different campuses.

The participants were all briefed together by the 'Spymaster', who explained that a spy ring in South Kensington had been compromised by a duplicitous double agent working for – gasp! – the Australian government. Teams needed to locate the five spies (played by students and obliging colleagues), hand over a key to the safehouse for a piece of intelligence and look out for clues to who might be the double agent. The teams circulated between the five 'spies' stationed at various locations (museums, a lab and the student bar) according to a timetable. Each spy then set the team a challenge to complete before handing over the intelligence (a puzzle piece) in exchange for a key. The end-game was to assemble the puzzle, which formed a picture of the Queen's Tower (one of the Imperial College buildings). Two of the most engaged players were dispatched to retrieve a suitcase from the Tower while the remaining players worked out the identity of the secret agent. The agent was arrested by campus security, and the players were awarded medals (ostensibly couriered over from Buckingham Palace).

Despite the game overall being very well received, timing was a problem. To avoid teams turning up simultaneously at a location, they were given rendezvous schedules cunningly disguised as bus timetables.

However, teams that were more effective or luckier at completing tasks were at a loose end between rendezvous, while others overshot their timeslots, and heavy rain meant that participants moved between venues more quickly than anticipated.

The game concept for 'The Mission' was inspired by playing 'The Accomplice'. Billed as a theatrical show through the streets of New York, 'The Accomplice' consists of the 'audience' being recruited to warn mobsters to leave town. Roles were assigned within the group – we were a mix of couples and family groups unknown to each other – and we were sent off to rendezvous with a series of characters (played by actors) who engaged in banter and set us puzzles to solve before sending us on our way to the next character and the ultimate showdown.

What made 'The Accomplice' so compelling was the willingness of the cast and the participants to 'create a scene': cast members were dressed in ridiculous clothing and shamelessly hammed up their performances in crowded public spaces, to the delight of participants and the amused bafflement of bystanders. One of the most memorable, and also controversial, aspects of the game was set in Chinatown. We had a fortune cookie that contained an instruction in Chinese. When we found someone to translate it, the instruction was to purchase a frog from a shop and take it to the next rendezvous point. We ended up ferrying a live frog through the streets of Chinatown, whereupon it was placed in a cooler box (frog welfare was catered for even if legitimate buyers might have had other catering ends in mind). Negotiating the streets of Chinatown with a live frog in an aerated bag is something one does not easily forget. Providing opportunities for memorable experiences, in which players find themselves in implausible situations but rising to the occasion to solve challenges, is at the heart of immersive play.

When I embarked on designing 'The Mission', I had in mind the way an immersive game can help make familiar environments feel full of wonder again. The game was commissioned by the Faculty Education Office for Medicine at Imperial College London, where staff had heard of the Medical Monopoly game that I organise each year (see Case Study 21). It was intended as a team-building event for the administrative staff who support teaching and learning across several campuses. Although the participants worked mainly in South Kensington, London, the majority had not entered the world-famous museums that line Exhibition Road for some time, if ever. When somewhere feels constantly available to us, we have a habit of indefinitely postponing visiting it. I wanted to create a sense of re-enchantment with the environment around the workplace. To do this, I focussed on three inadvertently alliterative elements:

people, place and puzzles. I will explore these elements in terms of designing immersive experiences and events, from both a game designer and a player perspective.

People: Players

Games that rely on participants' actions and cooperation resist easy classification because each player, and each group, will engage with the game differently depending on factors as unpredictable as mood, previous gaming experiences, and pre-existing relationships within a group. The game designer's challenge is to create an atmosphere that maximises the chances of a positive play experience. One of the main indicators of readiness to play is whether participants have voluntarily signed up to a playful event or whether they are there at the behest of others. Players who are there of their own volition might have higher expectations of the experience, especially if they have paid to participate. Those that are reluctant participants may be less willing to immerse themselves in the experience. One hopes, as a game designer, that the cynical will be converted once the game commences, but this is perhaps unrealistic. It is almost always preferable, in my experience, to cater for the eager in the hope that they will enthuse their more reluctant teammates, rather than insisting on full participation by everyone all of the time.

Game-based events in the workplace are often marketed to staff as being remedial in some way: to motivate staff to work effectively in teams, or enhance communication, or develop leadership skills. Staff who feel they already exhibit these abilities may be more resistant to this message than one that says, 'This is a break from work – come and have some fun!' – although the idea of fun at work may make others feel equally uncomfortable. When players engage in immersive play, there is a general expectation, or perhaps an apprehension, of being transformed in some way. This may account, in part, for the psychological anxiety that usually accompanies role play activities or team-building games: what might a change of role from 'professional' to 'player' reveal about our psyches, and will that show us in a good light? 'Imposter syndrome', in which people (typically women) consider themselves inwardly to be frauds (see, for example, Pedler, 2011) is thought to be widespread, and players may fear being 'exposed' in games that require quick thinking, ruthlessness or leadership. Ideas around 'permission to play' in a work environment are also explored in Chapter 6.

As a strategy for allaying fears about players revealing their 'authentic' selves in the company of those with whom appearances are usually carefully controlled, an immersive game can be very effective in creating a less threatening atmosphere of playfulness. If players take on roles, or personas, within the game, they are understood to be 'acting', and any slips into unbecoming behaviour (egotism, excessive competitiveness, impatience, or haplessness) can be attributed to the role, whereas behaviour that comes across as brave or clever can be claimed for oneself. By casting participants as 'spies' in 'The Mission', they were given a recognisable trope to inhabit that comes with permission for behaviours like being sneaky and subversive, bargaining and employing sarcasm. Although a spy theme might seem like an overworked cliché, it provides a heuristic that helps to do some of the scene-setting work when curating an immersive experience. At the outset, games designers should think carefully about themes and how they authorise different behaviours within a game, e.g. monsters, wizards, detectives, time-travellers and zombies. If there is no recognisable trope, players may need more scene-setting in terms of story so that they are clear about what role they are adopting. Roles, I would argue, are essential to immersive games. Merely being yourself does not afford the same potential for a memorable, transformative experience as investing the emotional energy into playing a role.

People: Playmakers

In game design, emphasis tends to be placed on the experience of playing the game, but equally important is the experience of participating as an actor or facilitator. To play the spies in 'The Mission', I recruited actors from the student drama society, roped in a willing colleague and persuaded my spouse to act as spymaster. All had to be willing to look a bit silly in public and to be confident enough to engage in improvised repartee with teams. We found that setting up a WhatsApp group considerably enhanced the experience for the facilitators. Actors in different locations were able to share impressions of levels of engagement of different teams, warn when teams were running ahead or behind schedule and generally engage in banter that enhanced the experience of involvement in the game. Some actors spontaneously engaged in character construction on the WhatsApp group, inventing elaborate backstories for their characters. Providing opportunities for this type of improvisation should be taken into consideration by games designers, as it generates immersion for facilitators as well as enhancing the performative elements of the experience presented to players.

People: Public

Challenges that involve members of the public in the open feel much riskier than those set indoors in private spaces, but they are also exciting. In 'The Mission', the teams were given a rendezvous point but still needed to identify the 'spies'. They were given a passphrase to say to the spy ('The purple penguin points to the southern cross only during the grapefruit season') to verify their credentials. There were some hilarious moments when teams thought they had identified the spy, communicated the passcode, only to be met with bafflement: they were speaking to an innocent member of the public. These unscripted moments are often the most-talked-about afterwards. Low-stakes 'failures' are part of the fun of immersive play in public settings.

Roping in members of the public often enhances their day as well as being fun for the teams. One 'Mission' actor was stationed on Exhibition Road, a busy tourist thoroughfare in London. With a stuffed kangaroo under her arm, the task she set teams was to be photographed with an Australian tourist. To complete the mission, teams needed to stop passing strangers and establish their nationality or persuade them to pretend to be Australian. In general, members of the public were only too pleased to be invited into the magic circle and become part of the game. The presence of the prop (toy kangaroo) helped to signal the gameful nature of the request and distinguished players from the evangelists, buskers and charity collectors that operate on Exhibition Road.

I have had similar success in organising 'duels' during team games. If play is taking place across a relatively small number of venues, a team may come across another team and challenge them to a duel. One duel involved finding a willing member of the public to accept a gift from the teams. Teams had five minutes to make or prepare a gift, and the recipient judged the gifts and awarded points accordingly. Teams were very enterprising at gift-making: works of art were knocked up from materials scavenged from the environment, and scratch choirs were assembled and quickly rehearsed. Poetry was written and performed. Crowds gathered and applauded. Participants surprised themselves with their ability to be creative at short notice.

There are potential risks with engaging the public, although these tend to be low. People may feel threatened or harassed or just annoyed at being approached. The way the invitation to play is extended is obviously crucial in this, and teams sometimes need to recalibrate their approach if they find they are being rebuffed. Members of the public are more likely to participate if they are not actively en route to somewhere, the activity does not take up much time, and the approach is friendly and polite. Written explanations of the activity are useful. When members of the public are given an envelope to open to reveal the task in which they are being invited to participate, they are far more likely to be willing to engage. Conceptualising this as an invitation rather than an instruction is also likely to be more successful.

Case Study 20: Heist! Help! (Giskin Day)

An immersive team game set in the Victoria and Albert Museum in London, which sees teams interacting with exhibits, finding clues and solving puzzles throughout the museum. It aims to develop team-building, problem-solving skills, communication and observation skills, while providing a fun activity over a few hours.

Players, in small teams, were sent a coded clue in advance, which told them to rendezvous with 'a shady lady in a scarf' in the museum cafe. She introduced herself as Sally Forth, the mistress of Shifty, a jewel thief. He is in jail but left a mysterious locked bag at her apartment. The bag may contain a priceless necklace or at least clues to where it might be. Or not. It is up to the team to see if they can solve the mystery. Sally leaves the bag and her phone number in case of problems (Shifty has a visit from his lawyer and there is a chance of tricking him into revealing some information). She goes off to pack her bags as she is fleeing the country.

The mysterious bag contained a series of nested locked bags and boxes, each of which was linked to a puzzle, each set in a different gallery in the museum. For example, there was a logic puzzle that required players to place plastic animals in the correct positions in a box based on clues involving ceramic animals on crockery in an exhibition, and a coded message was discovered by matching photos to gate decorations in the ironwork gallery.

By solving this series of puzzles over the course of three hours, teams can ultimately locate Shifty's treasure in a locker in the museum cloakroom and win the game. However, on one occasion a cloakroom mix-up led to one team being inadvertently handed a bag of laundry instead of the treasure. They searched through the laundry for clues for a while before realising something was amiss.

Figure 8.1 Solving logic puzzles in the Victoria and Albert Museum.
Credit: Emma Larsson.

Place

Organising games in public spaces makes it difficult, although not impossible, to leave physical clues in the environment. Fire Hazard Games, for example, run live action events in London in which physical letter drops often feature. However, one needs to be mindful of littering laws. Also, sticking clues on museum exhibits is viewed as vandalism, flyposting on the streets may lead to arrest and objects or clues may be appropriated (maliciously or not) by members of the public. Clues, therefore, ideally have to reside in extant objects or in people. Parks are generally viewed as playful places in which hiding and sneaking are less likely to be viewed with alarm than on a street. Ideally, a variety of physical environments is desirable in a game. For 'The Mission', I used South Kensington in London, with rendezvous spots in the Science Museum, the Victoria and Albert Museum, Exhibition Road, a laboratory in Imperial College and a bar – all locations within a short walk from one another. In designing the flow of the game, the distances between the venues had to be taken into account. As multiple teams were playing at the same time, they needed different itineraries to avoid walking in on other teams' interactions with the actors. Itineraries were provided in the guise of a 'bus timetable' to maintain the illusion of this being a secret mission.

It is a sign of the times that furtive behaviour may cause alarm; in major cities, we are surrounded by warnings about reporting suspicious behaviour. This can be problematic for hide-and-seek type games in which teams spy on each other or there is any kind of chasing involved. It is therefore advisable to signal that participants are 'players' by giving them hats or badges, or having them carry balloons (note that some public buildings ban helium balloons because they can set off smoke detectors if accidentally let go). Balloons on a stick are preferable, although some museums ban these too for no discernible logical reason. (I had to organise a car park attendant to act as balloon-sitting service for 'The Mission' teams while they were puzzle-solving in the Science Museum.) Montola and colleagues (2009) describe numerous cautionary tales of playful events in public ending in anger, chaos and, sometimes, court, where games designers have not been mindful enough of the psychological harm that can result when play mingles with real life. It is impossible to predict all the eventualities of playing in public environments, but it is the game designer's moral responsibility to anticipate where game elements may cause psychological or real harm to participants or bystanders. For that reason, scenes of violence or horror, unless very clearly signalled as a game, are best avoided.

Should one ask permission to run a game in a public museum or gallery? This can be a dilemma. You do not want to risk being refused, but you also do not want unwarranted interference if permission has not been sought. If the activity is designed to pose no risk of harm to visitors or exhibits and is likely to go unnoticed anyway, there is no imperative to officially seek permission from the institution. However, it may be polite to do so. This tends to involve putting something in writing to the duty manager or similar. A quick walk around the space in the hour preceding the activity to alert staff in the specific gallery or exhibition of what is likely to transpire can also forestall unwanted interference in the activity when it takes place. This is adequate for a one-off event, but those wishing to stage regular events are well advised to seek proper permissions. In my experience, museums and galleries tend to be welcoming of interesting activities taking place in their spaces, as long as the necessary assurances of safety are given and they do not interfere with or undermine activities and events organised by the institution itself. Sometimes, asking for permission can pay off. For 'The Mission', I asked to be allowed to place a clue in Imperial College's iconic Queen's Tower, more in hope than expectation. Not only was I allowed to do so, a member of security staff was allocated to unlock the tower when required, and the gameful guard also happily effected the arrest of the double agent during the denouement of the game.

Puzzles

The opportunity to solve puzzles is what transforms game players from being spectators to being participants. Puzzles should be designed to enhance the immersive nature of the game. This is achieved mainly through two means: first, being consistent with the theme of the game, and second, encouraging phenomenological engagement with the environment, by which I mean that puzzles should encourage physical activity rather than merely being intellectual. It is no coincidence that we use a tactile metaphor – 'feel' – to talk about internal emotions; the way our bodies encounter our environment has an effect on our emotional engagement. Good immersive games recognise this and aim for a varied, multisensory approach to engagement. One strategy is to keep pen-and-paper puzzles to a minimum in favour of challenges that involve behaviours (e.g. performances), communication and physical action. These need not be elaborate; simple engagement with props and locks are often enough to catalyse a sense of satisfaction when solved (see the 'Heist! Help!' Case Study).

As with all games, it is vital to pitch clues at an appropriate level of difficulty for the players: hard enough to be challenging but not so difficult as to engender frustration. Difficulty is tricky to gauge in advance, particularly when diverse teams are involved, so I recommend that hint systems are available. It assists with immersion when the hint system is in keeping with the theme. When an actor is involved, you can be quite ambitious with clues, because the actor can nudge participants if they are struggling. If actors are not part of the game, providing a phone number so that teams can call for help (to be dealt with in character) can be a good option. Providing QR codes for clues is also an option – provided the website to which players are directed is styled according to the theme and so becomes a seamless part of the game. This level of detail may seem excessive, but it is essential to continuously engage players' mindsets and maintain immersion, rather than players feeling that they are stepping in and out and in of the game.

Museums are great environments in which to set clues because objects and labels lend themselves to a range of types of puzzles (see Table 8.1 for some ideas).

Table 8.1 Ideas for clue types in museums and galleries

Clue type	Example	Solution
Cryptic clues linked to exhibits	'Keep your eyes peeled in Gallery 132 – you could be bowled over by this fruit'.	Find a glass bowl with a pattern of oranges: revealing a colour or number.
Photo matching and word counting	Photograph of part of an exhibit with a number (e.g. nine) written on the back.	Once the exhibit is located in the gallery, the number refers to the ninth word on the label. A sequence of these spells out a sentence.
Morse code	Series of questions on exhibits with yes/no answers.	Sequence of yeses/nos translates to dots and dashes to make up the Morse code for a word (supply a QR code linking to a decoder).
Telephone number	Locate objects and note their inventory/exhibit numbers.	Concatenate numbers to make up a phone number to text or call to receive a passcode by reply.
Pattern clue	Locate objects and note the path traced between them.	Path traced by moving between objects makes up the shape of a letter or number.
Object dominoes	Clues lead to a feature of an object (e.g. a sheep in a tapestry), which forms part of the clue to the next object (e.g. a sheepdog in a painting), which in turn has a feature linking it to something else, and so on.	Becomes a treasure hunt that culminates in final, significant object.
'Pitch' clue	Teams are given a mundane object (e.g. a feather) and asked to craft a pitch for it to be exhibited in the gallery.	Points awarded (ideally by a willing bystander) for the most convincing pitch.
Logic puzzle	Provide a box with compartments in rows and columns with props (e.g. plastic animals or fake flowers – each numbered or lettered). Clues themed around objects lead to correct placement of objects in the box. An example of a clue is 'The animal on the creamery jug in Case 12 should be placed below the animal painted on the pepper pot in Case 8'.	Certain compartments have a star. When objects are placed correctly, the ones in the starred compartments spell out a word or number (e.g. to a combination lock).

It helps with immersion if puzzles are in keeping with the theme. In 'The Mission', one of the actors played a hapless spy school student struggling to complete his Codes 101 assignment. He insisted on participants helping him to find the answers in the exhibition and using a codewheel before he would give up his 'piece of intelligence' (these were puzzle pieces that formed a picture when all the teams reconvened for the denouement). In a twist, the worksheet answer was a phone number to call, which was answered by another actor who pretended that players could be seen on CCTV and gave instructions to the team for some silly poses to strike. This sort of activity is a real litmus test of teams' willingness to go along with the playful agenda and provides facilitators with a gauge of how 'up for it' a team is at that stage of the game. The WhatsApp back channel was useful for communicating this information to other actors so that they could tailor their interactions to the gamefulness of the team.

Contingency or uncertainty, like ringing a phone number that may or may not have been worked out correctly, definitely adds to the excitement of a game. Including clues that involve chance (having a cost but with the promise of an unknown reward) increases the uncertain nature of a game, increasing motivation to engage (Malone, 1980). In points-based games, clues can be placed in envelopes; opening an envelope to reveal a clue or challenge can cost points, but players may earn points if they carry out the challenge.

Case Study 21: Medical Monopoly (Giskin Day)

Medical Monopoly is a game designed for use with medical humanities students at Imperial College to develop team-building skills and increase awareness of local museums and galleries. It is played and updated on an annual basis as an induction activity and takes a full day to play.

Players are divided into teams of five to eight people and allocated a Monopoly token as a team name (e.g. Top Hats, Battleships, Racing Cars). Challenges are set at 20 museums, galleries and exhibitions across London – anywhere that has free entry and sufficient medical content on which to set questions. Examples include the Royal College of Physicians museum in Regent's Park, the Saison Poetry Library, and the National Army Museum. Each team receives a backpack containing the 'board', a question booklet, as well as Chance and Community Chest cards. Venues are allocated monetary values according to the difficulty of the questions (e.g. the British Museum might be worth £50 and the Wellcome Collection £70). Teams accumulate virtual money (this acts as a score) by answering questions at each venue they manage to visit. A bonus amount is offered for gathering all the venues of the same colour. At the end of the day, teams gather for judging and prizes are awarded.

Play is enhanced by the random element provided by Chance and Community Chest cards. Chance cards are sealed in envelopes. Opening the envelope involves a 'fee' of £20, but teams could earn up to £100 by completing the challenge (e.g. filling out a death certificate for an exhibit in a museum). Community Chest cards provide challenges that can be completed during the game, e.g. £5 is available for a photograph of the team with a public defibrillator. One of the most entertaining challenges was for teams to film or photograph an imaginative way for a strawberry to die.

While overall the game was incredibly successful, museums exhibits change surprisingly frequently. A clue set on a page of an open book, for example, turned out to be obsolete, because the page was turned every few weeks to avoid fading. Overall, though, the game is worth the effort of organising as students find it memorable and a useful introduction to medical resources available across London.

Conclusion

Designing 'The Mission' was enthralling, time-consuming, entertaining, exhausting, exhilarating and nerve-wracking. Some players absolutely loved it and engaged with the game with enthusiasm and commitment. Others resented being hauled away from their desks for an afternoon when they had approaching deadlines and heavy workloads. Things went wrong. One of the student bars I had arranged as a venue announced it was closing early that day and I had to make a contingency plan at short notice. It rained incessantly throughout the event, meaning that teams moved between venues much more quickly than anticipated. As an immersive event, according to the criteria outlined earlier, 'absorption' and 'presence' were probably achieved more successfully than 'flow'. Moving between venues broke the immersion. With hindsight, I could have added some spying activities that would have maintained the immersive aspects of the game more effectively during these lag periods.

Making use of the real world as an immersive environment in which to play offers the advantages of a phenomenological experience that is, so far, unmatched by the digital world. The magic circle in the real world has a permeable boundary: members of the public can be invited in as participants in challenges or as spectators to a bit of theatre in their midst. Immersive games are not merely made in the moment, though. Talking through the game afterwards is just as much part of the experience as the event itself. It is then that the stories of play – triumphs and calamities – are shared and shaped. The experiences of others become part of the collective memory of an event.

Curating the right mix of surprise, risk, challenge, competition and reward is key to effective immersive game design. If the framework is in place with careful attention to people, place and puzzles, it makes room for improvisation within the bounds of the game. That is when the magic happens.

9   Building Playful Partnerships

David Woolley

Introduction

A playful approach to learning is rarely a solitary activity. The co-constructed nature of playful environments is part of the power of the venture. By building broader networks and coalitions, a playful approach can be significantly enhanced (Whitton, 2014). This chapter considers why external partnerships are important when designing playful events but also some of the more problematic areas associated with collaboration, including some of the ethical and legal aspects. To illuminate playful partnership, I will reflect upon the EduScape project, which is based on a partnership between a university and a school. Unlike many university-school partnerships, no remuneration or benefits are bestowed upon either party, yet each party gains.

A key element of partnership work or collaboration, call it what you will, is that everybody gets something out of it. In a post-feudal system this is usually in the form of monetary reward, however, with little available cash flowing in the education system post-austerity, seeking alternative rewards and benefits for participants is a worthy endeavour. Creating conditions of mutual benefit without a focus on money is interesting. After money, the next most highly valued 'currency' is time. Partnership work can consume more time than working within a single institution; relationship management and negotiating different protocols and vernaculars all takes time. So as recompense for a loss of time without the standard remuneration of money, collaborations need to create broader benefits.

This is where the playful aspect of playful partnerships becomes important. Just as a spoonful of sugar helps the medicine go down, a playful approach can make collaborations less testing. Working in partnership with a common goal across or within organisations harnessing a playful approach can lead to greater overall efficiencies. Time must be dedicated early on to foster this playfulness, but this can appear – from an external perspective – to lack direction and purpose. Permission to play becomes a key counter to this. Those within participating organisations must first be aware of the approach and see value in employing such an approach.

Second, the participants (or 'players') within the partnership need to want to play. Being forced to work in a playful way can be a very uncomfortable process. This underlines the need to establish the rules of the collaboration early on and set the tone that it will be playful in nature. Institutional and individual buy-in from the outset ensures a smoother playful collaboration.

Case Study 22: EduScapes (David Woolley/ Nicola Whitton)

Groups of sixth form students developed their own escape rooms to be showcased at a university conference. The partnership was between a university and a school sixth form. The collaboration aimed to explore, in context, how a playful opportunity to develop problem-solving would work within an academic sixth form environment and its impact on soft skills (and also a great chance to play some escape rooms).

We have been developing this model over a number of years and are currently in our third iteration of it. We originally started with 12 sixth form students in groups of four, with each team developing their own escape rooms. We now have a cohort of 40. The development model has adjusted over time, and we have found that the hard work has always been front-loaded at the start. The challenge has consistently been getting the teams to appreciate the task in hand (i.e. design and create an escape room that we can move from our sixth form to a university, which will be challenging enough to keep the brightest and the best occupied for 30 minutes while simultaneously being accessible to all).

To facilitate this, we have boiled down our inputs into the following discrete sessions:

1 Developing an understanding of puzzle typology.
2 Experiencing an EduScapes room (either one we had hashed together ourselves or one from a previous year).
3 Developing an understanding of the critical path for an escape room.
4 Experiencing a commercial escape room and then unpacking the game design of the room.

In our experience, if you do a great job with these four then the rest flows beautifully. The rest being paper prototyping, physical design, testing, design revision, testing, design revision, testing, design revision ... until you run out of time! The creativity in problem design we have seen from the students along with the co-development of their interpersonal skills has been truly remarkable.

Figure 9.1 Delegates playing an escape room at the Playful Learning conference.
Credit: Playful Learning Conference by Mark Power.

EduScapes: Escape the Classroom

The EduScapes project is in its third year and has consequently completed its third iteration of development. It is a collaboration between Manchester Metropolitan University (MMU) and Cheadle Hulme High School. The project is part of the enrichment cycle within the sixth form at Cheadle Hulme High School, which is showcased at the Playful Learning conference at MMU (see the Introduction and Chapter 3 for background on this conference). The project brief for students is to create an escape room within a very tight budget, with tight timescales. For the uninitiated, escape rooms are playful environments, traditionally in the form of a room (hence the name), whereby players are 'locked in' and have to solve puzzles and challenges to escape within an allocated time frame. Commercial escape rooms employ extensive theatrical backdrops to enhance the immersive nature of the room; thematic experiences are utilised and the room appropriately dressed. For instance, your team might have 60 minutes to escape before the sheriff comes back into town to arrest you for a crime you did not commit, or before a missile strike is launched, or before the release of a dangerous pathogen. You, as player, are charged with 'saving the day'.

As part of the brief, the EduScapes rooms are designed to be highly portable, usually broken down into two or three boxes that can be set up in almost any room. Commercial rooms operate on a somewhat larger budget than we as a secondary school can stretch to. This has led many teams to design scenarios based on the environment at hand: we have had disgruntled professors ready to blow up the university, various laboratory experiments gone wrong and office-based scenarios that take advantage of contemporary educational room layouts.

The rooms are designed to last for 30 minutes, must be portable and have explicit setup documentation so that they can be replicated elsewhere. In teams of four, students aged 16–17 design and make their own escape rooms. The teams compete against each other for the ultimate prize of EduScapes winner and to hold aloft the (chocolate) trophy!

The process of creating an escape room and starting with a blank sheet of paper presents a number of challenges, but before these are explored it is worth highlighting why this is a valid use of precious educational time. Developing critical thinking, creativity and problem-solving through team-working can often be highly contrived. Moreover, it can feel contrived and there is no getting away from the underlying agenda. A solution to this is often the use of outdoor education; setting scenarios whereby the whole team must work together for a common outcome is common practice. Bringing this back to classroom settings is more challenging. The EduScapes project takes the contrived nature of creative problem-solving through teamwork and asks participants to engineer a situation where problems must be solved through teamwork. It could be considered a meta-problem within and of itself.

Through our iterations of this project, we have been able to refine our practice to one that is replicable elsewhere. In essence, the success of the individual rooms is contingent on an effective launch of the project. Once students appreciate the scale and scope of the project, then they, largely, get on with it themselves. We have boiled down our initial inputs into the following discrete sessions, described in Table 9.1.

Much of this mirrors Walsh's (2017) model for room creation, which is a valuable practical guide of how to structure such work. After these stages, we then get the groups to conceptualise their rooms on paper. An initial evaluation of the room is then carried out with pointers and suggestions offered. We have tried different models with this partnership, with staff from MMU leading sessions versus being arbiters and evaluators. All approaches have demonstrated promise and show how flexible the partnership can be depending on other commitments.

Once conceptualisation is complete then the groups work largely independently on taking their rooms from the page and building them. This is followed by a significant testing phase where the teams play each other's rooms and invite friends and teachers to play (the change in dynamics being particularly noticeable in the latter case). This testing really allows the teams to appreciate the problematic nature of escape room design, as well as enabling the students to learn through safe failure and build resilience. We have found that the best rooms need to be tested at least 15 times, and it is at this point they are ready to be showcased.

Having external people play the rooms adds an important dimension to the testing process. MMU staff as part of the partnership are playing

Table 9.1 EduScapes induction as a four-step process

Step	Description
1. Developing an understanding of puzzle typology.	The best escape rooms get players to solve a variety of problems in a variety of ways to appreciate the scope and breadth of possible puzzles. To this end we run a session using different puzzle types as a competitive quiz: • Cipher • Logic puzzle • Crostic puzzle • Riddles • Odd one out • Code breaking • Pattern guessing • Crossword • Symbol substitution After the quiz we then unpack the actual nature of the puzzle and how these can be used. The puzzle types we used were deliberately chosen to be pen and paper activities to emphasise that elaborate staging was not needed to create a compelling and fun scenario.
2. Experiencing an EduScapes room	Having done this for a number of years, we have several rooms that we can play that demonstrate what can be done. It is really useful to get students to play other rooms so that they can see the minimum benchmark in terms of expectation. Where possible, we get them to play multiple rooms, as this allows them a greater appreciation of the possible variety and scope that is possible. During our initial run at the project we obviously did not have 'old rooms' to reuse and so had to make our own room up. While we were able to do this, our creation lacked the associated narrative and staging that the student-created ones have.
3. Develop an understanding of the critical path for escape.	Having had a go at an EduScapes room, we then get groups to attempt to recreate on paper the critical path for escaping the room. The dissection of the room in this way allows students to begin to deconstruct the process of room creation and consider the room from a conceptual perspective. By removing the staging and props and focusing purely on the problem-solving aspect of it, students begin to appreciate the relative complexity of different rooms and how this can be increased and decreased.
4. Experiencing a commercial escape room and then unpicking the game design of the room.	It is at this point in the process that we then take the students to experience a commercial room. We have played about with the order of this and taken them to a commercial room first, but we have found that the initial theoretical input in stages one and three really allows for greater appreciation of the sophistication of these rooms. An additional element of visiting commercial rooms is where possible asking room operators and room designers to come and speak to the groups about the design stage, room set-up and monitoring the game. Real stories from the field are invaluable to the process and inspire students.

with an eye to room development rather than their own personal enjoyment (although the experiences have been very enjoyable). This adds a useful element to the process where the students get to evaluate their rooms for different perspectives. The Playful Learning Conference has been hosted by MMU for the past three years, and the EduScapes project has been present each time. The EduScapes rooms allow conference delegates to play escape rooms at the same time as allowing the groups to interact with the public, albeit a public with a playful approach. The briefing and de-briefing element of EduScapes each time a room is played is where their teachers can really see the learning gains within the 'soft' curriculum.

It would be possible to run EduScapes as a single institution, provided sufficient time can be secured for devising and making escape rooms to be showcased and judging does not need external partners. However, we have found that by working across institutions, the difficulties and problems associated with collaborations have been more than countered. Having an external partner delivering and supporting playful sessions and workshops adds credence to the process. A-level students are delivered a very traditional academic diet, and opportunities for active play are limited. EduScapes gives permission for this play and provides ring-fenced time to work collaboratively to achieve a common goal. The sixth form curriculum is largely an individual endeavour for students, and EduScapes gives permission to co-create something innovative and problematic, which exists beyond an exam specification.

Most university-school partnership work is highly transactional in nature and is underpinned by monetary transfer in exchange for knowledge, training and/or accreditation. EduScapes is different. The time invested in the project by MMU adds academic standing and prestige to the project; it is not just messing about making an escape room, it is led by a professor and showcased at a large conference. From the university perspective, working with sixth form students and broadening their understanding of what universities can do is of great value, as well as the opportunity to highlight possibilities for innovative and meaningful curricula that are not exam-focussed. Further to this, being able to showcase the rooms at the conference creates an additional dimension to the playful world and enriches the delegate experience.

Case Study 23: Educational Escape Box (Andrew Walsh)

This playful approach was used in a higher education setting with various small groups of students at a time, especially international students. It aimed to introduce some basic facts about the university library and computing services in an informal, student-led way.

This case study describes the initial time I used this approach, which was a test bed for future use, although this method has now been used for a few different approaches, including learning about and evaluating different sources of information. As part of this experimental approach, I had a large wooden box made containing five different compartments, each of which can be padlocked. These could be opened by solving a series of puzzles (see http://gamesforlibraries.blogspot.co.uk/search/label/puzzles), which covered the same key facts and messages that are covered in our standard library induction. A set of library materials (e.g. leaflets, cards) was provided alongside, which could be investigated to find the correct answers.

The whole box was designed so that most groups could solve the puzzles within 30 minutes (which is how long library inductions normally last), and provision of clues meant that every group that tried it did solve it within the time limit (though some groups of staff that tried it needed more clues than any students did). When the final compartment was opened, sweets and badges were revealed as prizes, along with a congratulatory message.

A lightweight story ran underneath the whole experience and was threaded throughout the puzzles: a small number of 'evil librarians' were trying to prevent students from using the library resources, with the participants' main task being to help defeat these evil librarians.

The puzzles were fairly typical escape room-style puzzles, but they were all fairly straightforward and did not depend on high-level English language skills (no sneaky wordplay), so they were suitable for international students. We also ran the escape box with members of an autism lunch club, who appreciated that the approach taken to make it accessible to international students also made it widely accessible to other student groups.

The box went down well with every group we tried it with, and I have used the same idea since with other learning objectives.

The biggest mistake was the design of the box itself; making it large enough to be flexible for a range of puzzles, and sturdy enough to take some physical abuse from students, meant it was impractical to carry around – it was just too heavy!

Working with Partners

It is important to appreciate that when working with external partners this work is likely to be time-bound in nature. To rephrase the anonymously penned poem, partnerships happen for a 'reason, a season or a lifetime'.

While collaborative working over a lifetime is an unlikely endeavour, working for a reason or a season is far more common. Partnerships are usually founded to create efficiencies (Buys & Bursnall, 2007) and this does not in and of itself sound playful. The traditional mode of working with partners allows information to be shared more widely and tasks to be completed using multiple skills sets. Playful collaborations can also deliver these efficiencies through co-construction.

With partnerships founded for a reason or a season there inevitably is an outcome. The nature of this outcome determines the formality of the partnership. The more formal the partnership, the tighter the guiding principles need to be. Partnerships, where risk is associated by nature, should be constituted formally. For instance, if the outcome of a partnership is a publication or presentation, there is a reputational risk if the partnership is dissolved early. Memoranda of understanding aid in this and initial contracting in this area help all parties understand their roles and responsibilities (Ross et al., 2010). These vary in construction but essentially set out the road map of the partnership and the mutual expectations on all concerned parties. The more formal a partnership becomes, the more power dynamics come into play. Rules and structures are an inherent element of playful activities, and as such, this contracting can be done playfully and does not necessarily need recourse to the legal department. Much of this is through getting to know each other and attempting to fully appreciate each other's perspectives. Initially not focussing on the collaboration to come and developing trust through gameplay can lead to an accelerated and more effective contracting as interpersonal initial barriers are countered. For instance, in EduScapes we have found that the best way to engage additional partners is to get them to play EduScapes rooms with us. This truly breaks the ice and facilitates trust.

Firmly locating the partnership in a playful approach in low-risk collaboration is relatively simple. Where risks are introduced that impact on either party the dynamics of the partnership become more challenging; money, time and reputation are all facets which add tension to relationships. Mediating the risk of these elements from the outset is key to ensuring a smooth and successful partnership. By outlining to all parties what is at stake and the implications of failure or delay, this facilitates a trusting and purposeful relationship (Ross et al., 2010). Longer lasting relationships are founded on trust earned over time. As collaborations extend over time, creep in the remit of the partnership frequently occurs (Kalir, Fahy, Kupperman, Schiff, & Stanzler, 2018). This leads to ongoing and persistent renegotiation of partnership boundaries and remits. Much of this is due to the lack of full appreciation of each other's wants and needs. Hence, the initial playful contracting is critical to successfully outlining the needs of each partner for the reason or the season.

Maintaining a collaboration between two or more external partners over time without formal commitments of money can be challenging.

Standard project management protocols and tools that keep the commercial and business world on track are unsurprisingly applicable in playful approaches. They may not sound playful, but there is nothing more fun than following the rules! Planning and mapping out milestones throughout the life of a project is crucial. Moreover, regularly revisiting these milestones and utilising the trust that has been fostered to accurately assess progress to date allows future plans to be meaningful. There are mechanisms that can be used, which can add a frisson to the proceedings to engender a more playful approach. For instance, carrying out project management meetings in a virtual game environment (Owens, Davis, Murphy, Khazanchi, & Zigurs, 2009) and assigning avatars to each participant is a far cry from poring over a Gantt chart. Other digital collaborations such as shared online documents move the partnership to a co-construction, becoming less about holding to account and more about ways forward. Of import throughout the process is a clear understanding of roles and responsibilities throughout the lifecycle of the project. Extending the avatar concept still further, creating character description sheets with 'missions' to be completed and timescales for this is a way to carry out project management, task delegation and ascribing timescales in a playful way.

As this section began by saying, most collaborations exist for a reason, a season or a lifetime. It is important to acknowledge this and celebrate it. The successful completion of a project should be marked in an appropriate way. Partnerships are inherently a social construct and the usual and normative forms of celebration are always permissible. Simply acknowledging a job well done and being proud of the partnership's achievement is a minimum. However, in our experience successful playful collaborations beget further playful collaboration. The scope and scale of the work grows, and through successive successful cycles of working together project work of this nature is less alien. Indeed, we have found this transition leads to wanting to collaborate on other projects and support each other in different ways – the reason becomes the season and, who knows, maybe a lifetime.

Working with Children and Young People

The school curriculum in England is already packed full to bursting; there is too much to teach and too little time. Approaches that allow for multiple areas of the curriculum to be addressed are always welcome. Furthermore, being able to address both the 'hard' curriculum of subject content alongside the 'soft' curriculum of social skills, problem-solving, oracy and resilience is always welcome. Playful approaches, when used appropriately, can do this. It is important when developing playful approaches within the curriculum to have a clear rationale of why playful approaches are being used and what is actually trying to be taught. Just because a session happens to mention the chemical name for salt does not mean that chemistry is being taught. It is perhaps being used in a non-domain specific way, which is fine, but it is not being taught. While a treasure hunt involving chemical names, symbols and definitions allows content to be explicitly learnt, problems to be solved and team work to be fostered.

With a focus on the 'hard' curriculum, in England the Early Years Foundation Stage (EYFS) is a child-centred approach largely consisting of child-initiated learning. Much of this is carried out through exploration and play. EYFS specialists are adept at turning seemingly any play scenario into a teaching point rooted in the curriculum. This approach gradually tails off throughout Key Stages 1 and 2 (ages 5–11 years), and by the time children enter secondary school at the age of 11, the majority of academic learning centres on desk-based activities with the teacher expounding from the front. That is not to say that playful approaches are not harnessed; classroom games can be and are utilised well. Playful approaches usually foster high levels of engagement, but this must not be seen as a proxy for learning (Whitton & Moseley, 2015). The efficiencies in learning associated with the teacher talking from the front of the room and interactively questioning are significant. It would appear that we are trying to set up a dichotomous situation here of play vs. teaching in the secondary school, and this is not the case. Whether the teacher chooses to expound from the front or establish small groups of play is not important. Both can be achieved through playful approaches and the associated 'soft' curriculum can be enhanced and delivered (Lopata et al., 2005).

Leading the play carries with it notions of power and influence. Whoever leads the playful approach must at all times remember that children and young people are more vulnerable than adults. Through play, vulnerabilities can be exposed, and it is the responsibility of the leader to be cognisant of their statutory safeguarding duties. Play therapy is a growing field with a relatively new body of academic research. Unlike talking therapies, play therapy takes advantage of the developmental and maturational differences between children and adults (Bratton, Ray, Rhine, & Jones, 2005). Through play, emotional difficulties can be unearthed within a structure which is at the same time safe and purposeful. In these situations, the safeguarding responsibilities of all involved need to be understood, and it is important to acknowledge that while safeguarding themes are common across different areas, each institution may have different interpretations of them. As such, it is imperative to understand the local position and policy before entering into play that may prompt disclosures.

Case Study 24: Adventures in Education (Giskin Day)

This prop-and-prompt game was the first activity for staff grouped into new educational communities of practice (eCOPs) at Imperial College School of Medicine in 2017. It was designed as a team-building activity and to provide an opportunity to think reflectively and innovatively about the purpose and practice of eCOPs.

Each team received a picnic basket containing a series of prompts (activities to do) and props (craft materials and seaside-themed objects); see Figure 9.2. A large map of an island formed the field of play. Activities included everyone crafting a boat with a collectively-designed sail. Teams then discussed the 'landscape' of their plans for developing their eCOPs. They wrote messages about their expectations and placed them in a bottle to be revisited in three months' time. Artificial snow was provided. Making it snow on their island created the opportunity to discuss what happens when the going gets tough. To round off the activity, there was treasure to be found in a treasure chest. One team decided that the treasure was 'each other' before discovering an actual treasure chest under their table.

Figure 9.2 An exciting picnic basket full of props.
Credit: Giskin Day.

Conclusion

Successful playful collaborations are highly effective when all involved parties are approaching the work from the same position. Where there is a difference in understanding, difficulties can arise. Intellectual property (IP) is a large element of this. When working playfully with a desired outcome there is a co-constructed element of the project. The overall ownership of this can be contested. If the partnership is truly collaborative, then the project could not be completed without the involvement of all parties, and hence it is not unreasonable to assume a shared ownership and credit. However, this is an assumption and does not take into account the nuanced nature of partnership work and co-construction. It is vital that IP is taken into account before project commencement, ideally in the contracting or 'rule creation' element of the work. While this may sound overly officious, if there is any chance of the project being monetised or published for wider esteem and appreciation, then an understanding of how each party benefits is crucial. Equally, discussions about credits on academic outputs (e.g. order of names on a journal article) are useful to have up front.

To add complexity to this, it is also worth considering sponsorship or external funding. Sponsors or funders of collaborative projects do so for a variety of reasons, and when done fairly all parties benefit. There are various elements to consider when establishing a sponsorship agreement: exclusivity, payment, benefits, exit clause and intellectual property. Exclusivity refers to the number of sponsors a project may wish to attract; will there just be one sponsor or more? Being clear on this from the outset reduces potential stumbling blocks moving forwards. Payments and benefits are just those; they underpin the transactional nature of the sponsorship. Being clear on who gets what for what and when is the crux of any sponsorship agreement. Termination of a sponsorship agreement is also worth considering. Collaborations that are for short, time-bound events, such as conferences, have an implicit termination element. However more complex ongoing partnerships may not be as clear-cut, and consideration of notice period or out-of-pocket payments/benefits are worth considering. Finally, sponsorship within intellectual property debates is challenging. It is imperative that discussion of who owns any work product is discussed. The output of collaborations under sponsorship can be considered to be jointly owned. Hence it is imperative to detail expectations around this from the outset. It is best practice and certainly advisable where sponsorship is involved to have a sponsorship agreement in writing so that all discussions you have are clearly recorded. For larger or potentially more complex collaborations with or without sponsorship, it is always advisable to seek legal advice to ensure you are fully informed.

Despite the potential risks, practical issues that need to be considered and potentially time-consuming nature of external collaborations, we are convinced that they offer great value to playful learning events and experiences. Particularly when approached playfully, with a spirit of adventure and exploration, openness and a willingness to collaborate and share ideas, outputs and outcomes.

10 Designing Conference Games

Katie Piatt

Introduction

A conference game is an activity or activities that pervade the conference. Unlike a single icebreaker or presentation, it provides a playful path through the conference where delegates can participate in as little or as much as they wish. You typically play as yourself in a conference game, unlike immersive games where you assume a role separate from reality. Previous chapters have discussed having a playful approach to event planning, but this chapter considers the inclusion of a game at the centre of the conference design.

A well-designed conference game can help delegates to increase their engagement during the conference and can provide deeper understanding of content or increase networking opportunities; while allowing delegates to choose when and how to participate.

In this chapter, I will explore two conference game case studies in depth: the Playful Learning 2016 Marbles and Missions game and the Mahara 2014 Leaderboard game. I will look at the design considerations for whole conference games, practical issues to consider and ways to increase engagement of delegates through the game. I will reflect on these two examples to provide practical tips and advice and present a series of steps to help you design your own conference game.

Designing Marbles and Missions

The first Playful Learning conference in 2016 commissioned a game to add a game layer throughout the conference in keeping with the general philosophy of the event (see Chapter 3 on organising a playful event). A hundred people were anticipated, and a small budget was available for the game design.

Case Study 25: Marbles and Missions (Katie Piatt)

This game used marbles as currency throughout the conference, which could be traded or earned by completing challenges. By using a physical currency, we aimed to provide a tactile points system to keep delegates engaged throughout the conference. Marbles were identified as a cheap, easily obtainable item that also felt sufficiently playful to use as a theme and mechanic for the game. We devised a series of games and challenges, all of which gave players the opportunity to win and trade marbles. The games were designed to enable players to experience a range of emotions associated with play, for example: risk, fear, awkwardness and excitement.

On arrival, delegates took part in a marble run challenge at registration to earn their first marbles and this set the tone for the conference. This worked well apart from those arriving late who were keen to just get registered without the delays of having to play a game to win marbles. A game of Pass the Parcel with marbles as prizes was used before the opening keynote as an icebreaker.

Participants were invited to sign up for text messages to receive personalised text message challenges throughout the conference, such as: 'take a photo of your marble dressed up' and 'win a game of rock, paper, scissors to win a marble'. These challenges were well received but intensive to manage in terms of recording which challenges had been sent to which players. At any time, players could trade up their marbles for better marbles, for example, five small marbles for a galaxy marble.

To end the conference, a final 'risk everything' challenge was devised, where anyone willing to place all their marbles in the hat had a chance of winning all of them. This had good participation and truly raised the stakes at the end of the conference.

Figure 10.1 Marbles were a precious commodity at Playful Learning 2016.
Credit: Jen Pacheco.

Designing the Game

Schell (2008) talks about the "Lens of Economy" (p. 204), how your players can earn or buy currency and when that is an effective technique. A desirable form of 'currency' such as beads, stickers or trading cards can help delegates keep motivated at an event. We identified marbles as our currency: nostalgic, easily obtainable and tactile; and also felt sufficiently playful to use as a theme and mechanic for the game. We devised a series of games and challenges, both physical and online, all of which gave players the opportunity to win and trade marbles. The games were designed to enable players to experience different feelings associated with play, e.g. risk, fear, awkwardness, excitement.

The audience for the conference were those with an identified interest in playfulness, which allowed a level of risk and pervasiveness for the game design higher than might otherwise be recommended or possible (compared with the Mahara conference, below; and see Chapter 4). Where you consider this level of playfulness is a step too far for your own audience, it is recommended to scale back by selecting a smaller set of elements and removing elements which you consider more risky.

Practical Issues

When planning the game, we considered integration to match the main touchpoints of the conference – e.g. registration, keynotes, breaktimes, etc. The first challenge, a homemade cardboard marble run, was set up before the main registration desk: delegates had to play the game to win marbles before moving onto the more formal conference registration. The marble run was a traditional roll the ball type of game, delegates were given five marbles to roll and the board had a series of holes, each of differing values into which they had to try to get their marbles to fall (see Figure 10.2). Their score then converted into marbles, which could be used for trading and further play during the three days. Logistically, this added an extra step to registration, which although fun did cause delegates who were arriving close to the start time to just want to get on with it.

During the conference there were continuous marble challenges such as 'take a photo of your marble outside' or 'dress up your marble'. Each completed challenge won the player more marbles, which could be traded through a member of the games team; the mechanics of trading reminding players of their childhood: trading up for better or bigger marbles. The challenges culminated during the final keynote, where willing players risked their collected marbles for a chance to win them all.

The marble game was staffed by three people, covering all of the activities outlined above. This ensured the team would also have time to take part in the conference itself and support each other when responding to

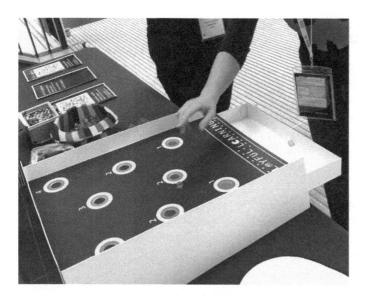

Figure 10.2 Playful pinball with marbles.
Credit: Playful Learning Conference by Mark Power.

events – such as treasure hunt clues going missing! Running a game entirely on your own would give no opportunity to also enjoy the conference content and be a much more stressful experience if any issues arose.

Points of Engagement

Marbles, as a nostalgic, collectable resource, seemed to capture the delegates' interest: they took photos and tweeted about their growing collections. This all added to the social media buzz around the event, which in turn raised the stakes, as players could see how other players were progressing which helped to maintain interest. The inclusion of a few compulsory activities, such as pre-registration, ensured that all delegates were aware of the game and were involved automatically (with a starting currency), removing a barrier to entry if delegates have to choose or complete an additional optional activity in order to take part.

Mahara 2014

The University of Brighton hosted the national Mahara (ePortfolio software) UK conference in 2014 for roughly 100 delegates over two days. The conference team designed a game to illustrate the playful approach the Brighton team takes to their work.

Case Study 26: Leaderboarding the Mahara Conference (Katie Piatt)

The University of Brighton hosted the national Mahara UK conference in 2014 for roughly 100 delegates over two days. The conference committee wanted to add some playful elements to the event to make it stand out. We implemented a conference game using a leaderboard that was designed to encourage socialisation amongst delegates.

The leaderboard tracked delegates' engagement with a series of challenges based around the use of Twitter and an online quiz. The game generated moderate levels of engagement (27% of delegates participated in the challenges beyond merely tweeting about the conference), received positive feedback and achieved high levels of amplification for the event through social media (the conference hashtag trended on UK Twitter).

Key lessons learned were to:

- Integrate the game closely into the conference agenda and scheduled events to achieve increased participation rates.
- Retain the motivation of participants and eliminate unwanted gaming behaviours (such as cheating) by modifying the scoring metrics as the game progresses.
- Ensure the rules and scores are transparent and regularly reiterated to participants.
- Manage the timing of game updates and activities to create anticipation and to allow participants to concentrate on the content of the conference during presentations and break-out sessions.

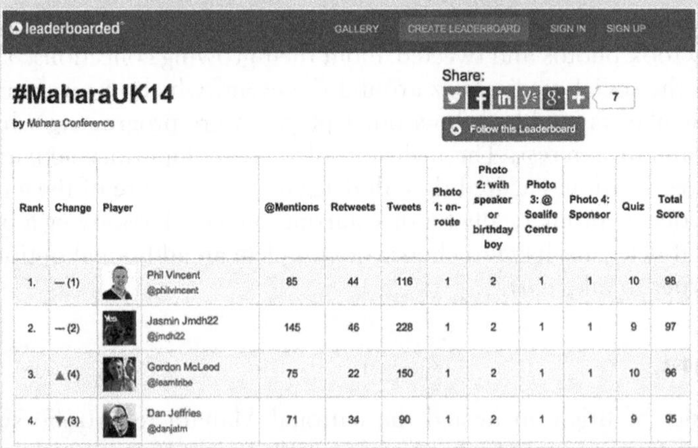

Rank	Change	Player	@Mentions	Retweets	Tweets	Photo 1: en-route	Photo 2: with speaker or birthday boy	Photo 3: @ Sealife Centre	Photo 4: Sponsor	Quiz	Total Score
1.	— (1)	Phil Vincent @philvincent	85	44	116	1	2	1	1	10	98
2.	— (2)	Jasmin Jmdh22 @jmdh22	145	46	228	1	2	1	1	9	97
3.	▲ (4)	Gordon McLeod @leamtribe	75	22	150	1	2	1	1	10	96
4.	▼ (3)	Dan Jeffries @danjatm	71	34	90	1	2	1	1	9	95

Figure 10.3 Engaging delegates with a conference leaderboard.

Credit: Katie Piatt.

Designing the Game

As the organisers of the event, there were no limitations on how the game could link into the conference. Expecting extensive use of social media at the conference, particularly Twitter, we decided to use a leaderboard to award points to encourage socialisation amongst delegates. All activity was based around this very visible online leaderboard. Players primarily earned points by tweeting, being retweeted and replies received to their tweets using the conference hashtag #maharauk14. There were also four photo challenges to complete and a 'Super Tricky' quiz.

We saw promoting the game and making it part of the conference as key for high engagement. The welcome to the delegates included the game introduction. Updates to the leaderboard were released at each break in the conference (morning coffee, lunch, etc.), which provided anticipation and removed distractions during the presentations. The quiz was made available several days before the conference began, but the quiz scores were not added in until the morning of the second day, allowing more time for completion and a sudden jump in scores. A student helper was recruited in order to assist with the manual scoring elements, such as confirming if a photo challenge had been met.

The selected software provided many display options, making it easy to embed the leaderboard onto our event website, link to it, project on the main stage, etc. – giving it high visibility. The software could automatically calculate the points and leaderboard positions based on our selected weightings for each criterion. Twitter scores could be polled on demand, and challenge scores could be manually added through the software.

Practical Issues

The automated nature of the leaderboard software allowed the game to be primarily run by one person, however, due to some manual checking of challenges, a student helper was recruited to assist on day two to update scores and check who had completed quizzes. Updates to the leaderboard can be automatically released, but in order to maximise engagement these were released manually at lunch and break times.

In order to keep everyone interested, we wanted to ensure the players at the top of the leaderboard changed regularly. Using the different weightings on each of the metrics we were measuring allowed this kind of manipulation. Before the conference, tweets counted heavily; during day one, the photo challenges were weighted more heavily; on day two, the quiz was weighted; and then for the final release, the metrics were more balanced out to provide an overall winner. Players could see their scores on each of the challenges, but they could not see the weightings of the metrics. This did not cause any issues but did create a strong sense of anticipation at each break in order to see their new position on the leaderboard.

Points of Engagement

The Participation Inequality rule (Nielsen, 2006) states that typically 10% of participants get partially involved in participative activities such as this and 1% get fully involved. For MaharaUK14, we saw over 10% getting fully involved (doing every challenge, 13 out of 120 delegates) and 27% getting partially involved (doing at least one 'challenge' over and above tweeting). These high levels of engagement achieved equally high levels of amplification for the event through social media (the conference hashtag trended on UK Twitter).

We observed that the delegates seemed particularly responsive to the game activity. Many delegates knew each other and saw the conference as an enjoyable networking event in Brighton already, so were in the right frame of mind to take part. It was also important that the game was integral to the event, introduced at the beginning and updated frequently in line with programmed breaks so that it was more than an ancillary activity.

The two case studies above provide examples of activities that might inspire your own conference game. Looking back at the common elements that worked well, we can identify a low barrier to entry as a critical design feature. Handing out marbles on arrival or automatically scoring tweets turned conference delegates into game players before they even knew there was a game – moving the game forward from there was then relatively easy. These two examples also both present opportunities for building up to more complexity or pulling back to make the games low risk depending on your audience. As gamemaker, you have control of this as your event proceeds, so do not be afraid to change your plans as you respond to the audience. Finally, ensure you get to enjoy the game by making sure you have colleagues or helpers to discuss changes and help keep score or run elements for you. It is always good to be able to step back and observe how your game is working and if it achieved all that you had hoped.

Case Study 27: LILAC Top Trumps (Rosie Jones)

An adaptation of the Top Trumps card game, in which players have to compare selected attributes of an object, was used as an icebreaker with delegates at the opening of LILAC 2017. The game offered a chance to encourage delegates to find memorable talking points that, while loosely conference-related, could spark new topics of conversation. Using a relatively familiar technique, it was easy for all to engage with.

Before the opening keynote, blank Top Trump cards were distributed. These had the following categories:

- Loyalty (how many times a delegate had attended the conference before).

- Commitment (how long it had taken them to get to the conference).
- Influence (how many twitter followers they had).

The presenters showed an example of their own Top Trump cards, and then the audience were asked to get into pairs and complete their partner's card for them. There was then an opportunity to determine who in the audience had the greatest numbers, for which they won prizes. The delegates responded really well to this activity and it offered talking points throughout the conference. In particular due to one participant spending days travelling there.

Steps to Design Your Own Conference Game

When beginning to design your own conference game, I suggest a series of considerations around three game design themes:

- Culture – the context of your game.
- Play – the experience of your players.
- Rules – the formal game design.

Step 1: Culture

This section provides a series of prompt questions on the players, context and constraints for your game to help you start planning. Although obvious, a high-tech activity will not work without Wi-Fi, and a fancy dress challenge might crash and burn at a senior corporate summit – so consider the following points carefully:

- When planning a conference game, first of all consider the culture of your players – what unites them, what common interests do they have and are the delegates attending your conference likely to respond well to a game? This will help you decide how much playful activity is appropriate and how challenging you want to make it. The first case study above took advantage of a known playful audience, but you can contrast this with the second example of a more social media savvy audience to work out how to pitch your own game.
- What is the context for your event? Is there a history of common activities, themes or approaches for the conference that you can draw on? Are you able to integrate the game into the programme of the conference, or is this a supplemental activity? If possible, integrate the game closely into the conference ideals, aims, agenda and events. Depending on the context, you might decide to just have some timetabled standalone activities or to embed a full playful layer as described earlier.

- This understanding of culture is important if you want to achieve increased participation rates. It is likely that attendees identified with at least some of these cultural traits when booking on the conference, and so you are likely to work within the right cultural context.
- What constraints are there at your event? If players are not likely to have access to Wi-Fi or have their own devices, then you may need to rule out online activities. If you happen to have access to large outdoor spaces, your game might make use of them (hide and seek, anyone?).
- Does the use of particular game mechanics – such as competition or visible leaderboard/points – work with the identified context? At the second Playful Learning conference, delegates were requested to bring cuddly toys (see Case Study 11); this works well where delegates are anticipating the experience but could backfire if delegates see the activity as unrelated to their reason for attendance and do not comply, leaving a small group of players feeling isolated. Getting this balance right is key: your aim is to find a way to make the game fun but still keep it relevant enough to players for them to want to engage.
- Social media can be a good way of capturing and promoting game activity. Do your players Tweet, use WhatsApp or Instagram? Are you able to use the main conference hashtag? If this is possible, then we recommend you do use it rather than trying to get activity going on a separate hashtag, which can be confusing for players.
- Is there opportunity to have a physical focus for your game such as a central projection of a leaderboard, a marble distribution desk or a locked box (see Case Study 32) as a focal or gathering point? This gives players somewhere to talk about the game activity and recognise other players (and gamemakers) more easily.
- If you have budget available for the game, do you want to consider buying or creating any game artefacts such as marbles or custom trading cards? Players tend to like physical objects, but these often require a long lead time for ordering and can be expensive if you are creating a bespoke object for a small number of players. Piloting simply one year, then building into a budget for subsequent years, is a good way to approach this.
- How much support do you have for the game? Are you on your own, in which case activities need to be simple to run, or have you got colleagues available, which allows you to be more responsive and have manual elements, such as scoring, for your game?

Step 2: Play

Now that you understand the content, you need to think through the experience you are creating for your players – how will this game work? Schell (2008) uses lenses to help focus your thinking. Through his "Lens of Essential Experience", you should ask yourself what kind of experiences you want the player to have, how essential that is and how to ensure your game captures the essence of that experience.

- As you design your activities, you should playtest on both willing and (ideally) unwilling volunteers, well before the event, and continually refine your designs. I am guilty of designing puzzles that are too hard – they make perfect sense to me but stop the fun for anyone else. Through testing and refinement, you can work out the optimal level of 'hint' to help players enjoy your challenges.
- As far as possible, activities should relate to the conference content: photo challenges of delegates or objects, quizzes about the content of the conference, etc., and not be completely separate. A good way to achieve this is to find a theme you can identify that fits with the conference ethos or focus and work around that. Of course, if you get the opportunity you may be able to set a theme and then use that for the game and have it supported by the rest of the conference – everyone loves a pirate theme, I have found!
- Be careful that you do not bite off more than you can chew – it is easy to overcomplicate the activities in your game. There is a temptation to design too many activities with layers of gameplay going on. Remember, delegates are also attending a conference, and the game should complement, not replace or confuse. It is disheartening when you realise the players did not even see the puzzles you had created for them because your design was so subtle and cryptic. The rule is to keep it simple!

Step 3: Rules

The final step is to ensure your game makes sense, is fair and will work in practice, so you need to think through the logistics and rules.

- Have a framework so that everyone knows when key events or actions are needed, but ensure you are able to adapt as you go once the game is implemented without upsetting delegates. This is important to keep everyone engaged and not risk being accused of favouritism or lack of clarity.
- A lesson we learned from the above events is that the perception of fairness is all-important. At times during the conference, players asked us to confirm that their photo challenge points had been logged correctly, and as these points were visible, it enabled them to be sure their scores were correct. Awarding of points, prizes, etc. can be playful and a little frivolous/random, but attendees will want to see some logical reasoning and fairness behind them.
- Retain the motivation of participants and eliminate unwanted gaming behaviours by modifying the scoring metrics as the game progresses, if needed. Ensure the rules and scores are transparent and regularly reiterated to participants.

- Manage the timing of game updates and activities to create anticipation and to allow participants to concentrate on the content of the conference during presentations and break-out sessions.
- What do you want to do if players are late to the game – can they still join in? Do they have any chance to catch up? A way of letting them play despite missing earlier elements helps get them engaged in the conference quickly.

Conclusion

The core idea presented in this chapter is of creating a 'playful path' through your conference at the centre of the conference design. The aim is to create a theme that fits well with the conference culture and ethos and to ensure everyone is included automatically and easily at the start. This provides a strong base to help your delegates to engage with each other, to accept the playful theme alongside engaging with the conference content, and to give them further opportunities to get involved through play. Through the two case studies of fully pervasive conference games, I hope to have inspired readers to follow the three steps outlined to plan, test and implement their own designs.

Part V
Playful Practice

11 Playful Presentations

Alex Moseley and Rosie Jones

Introduction

The freedom to incorporate play into presentations is often inhibited by the practical constraints of the environment. Playful activities are easier to deliver in a flexible, informal setting, and this often means they are avoided in a more formal rigid space. Movement, hands-on and collaborative activity can be prohibited by a lecture theatre setting. The limitations of the traditional lecture theatre environment are clearly highlighted by a wave of new lecture theatre developments. It also should be noted that lecture theatres often encourage a particular type of behaviour "… as soon as students enter the room they know what is expected of them" (Graetz & Goliber, 2002): both a positive (familiar, comforting) and negative (normalising didactic teaching) reflection on the space.

Expectations of how a presentation event like a keynote is delivered can prohibit playful adoption. There are few examples of keynotes delivered in a playful way, and these can therefore be seen negatively by delegates who have set expectations of a keynote form. "Games instead of a presentation? Would my line manager think it was worth allowing me to attend? I can guarantee not" (a direct quote from feedback at LILAC, referring to a playful keynote). Keynotes are also usually strictly time-constrained, and playful activities (indeed, anything that involves the audience) can be unpredictable in their timing. The occasion of a keynote can therefore be a daunting environment in which to experiment, particularly as they are usually a one-off or relatively rare occurrence for a presenter and as such come with the pressure to do well and to boost reputation. There can also be a fear of losing control or not covering the whole content.

However, if we turn to the space itself, a lecture theatre affords the occasion to perform, to engage a large audience and to take advantage of high-quality audio-visuals. Why not therefore use this ideal setting for an interactive performance that also reinforces learning: "place […] should not restrict them from including some form of interactive element in a session" (Jones, Peters, & Shields, 2007, p. 36). Ideas around 'flipped learning' can be adopted, where the session is inverted so that participants have the materials in advance and the environment can be used for further learning and problem-solving, which opens up space for more playful approaches.

Case Study 28: 'Choose Your Own Adventure' Lecture (Katie Piatt)

Typically, presentation software is designed to be run in a linear style with the tutor in control. However, by incorporating voting, you can allow students choices on which content should be covered next, having prepared slides to cover all anticipated options. By giving students some agency about what happens next in the classroom, you can provide engagement as well as some interaction.

At the University of Brighton, we have a license for Nearpod, an interactive presentation tool that allows slide presentations controlled by the tutor, as well as voting, content embedding and drawing activities. Where this software is not available, PowerPoint can be used in a similar way, replacing the electronic voting with any other tool or a simple show of hands in class. This technique can be used in a range of situations, including undergraduate teaching, staff training and for conference presentations.

A good model is to divide the content you want to cover into four or five main areas. Create a voting slide giving these as options, with a tempting label for each chunk of content. Ask the students to vote and then jump to the prepared slide covering the content for that section. A useful tip is to put 'bookmark' slides into your slide deck so you can clearly see where to go, and the viewers need never see this slide. Once that content is complete, return to your voting slides and ask what to cover next.

Tip: always allow a 'wildcard' option; it is always a surprisingly popular choice and gives you room to add in something unexpected, such as a playful activity.

This idea originated with Dr Rebecca Graber at the University of Brighton and is gratefully acknowledged. She has created a research methods session using this technique, allowing the students to dictate which areas they want to cover in the class, making choices of the methodology or research approach for example.

Constraints (and How to Use Them to Your Advantage)

The first thoughts entering the mind of most teachers, trainers or speakers who are facing a presentation within a lecture room turn to the limitations of that space. Jones and colleagues (2007) suggest, rather, that one should address the type of activity first and then how to deliver this in a constrained environment. We have all experienced large-group presentations ourselves: we know what it is like to be stuck halfway along the middle row, watching a screen and a more-or-less-engaging speaker for an hour or more. The space is both constrained (personally) and massive (spatially); there is limited scope for interaction; and the screen tends to dominate the 'teaching' space. There are also the constraints of the occasion: often large-group presentations have an expectation of formality and information-heavy content.

In games design, when constraints are present (in, say, the limitations of a digital platform, or the age level the game is aimed at), these often become a design feature or challenge that the games designer *designs to meet*. This was most prevalent in early digital game development, when graphics, colours, memory and processor power were extremely limited – yet some highly creative games developed out of those limitations. Even today, designers are either imposing or using constraints to encourage creativity (Kultima, Alha, & Nummenmaa, 2016). Indeed, the very nature of playing a game is to accept rules and constraints: Suits (1978) describes this as a *lusory* attitude: and describes how the constraints imposed by golf (different clubs, terrain, weather, bunkers, penalties) make it enjoyable to play. As opposed to simply picking the ball up, walking to the hole and dropping it in: no constraints, but also no enjoyment or skill.

Why not, therefore, see the limitations and constraints imposed by the 'presentation' as an opportunity for good design and heightened engagement: in the same way that game design uses them to create enjoyable, engaging experiences? In the rest of this section, we will take each of the main constraining elements of large group presentations and turn them into design challenges. For each, we will draw on our own – and others' – experience of designing and delivering presentations to provide practical examples of playful design solutions.

The 'Amphitheatre' Constraint

Participants arranged in long rows (limited movement) or on many tables in a flat space (enforced groupings) where the 'performance' takes centre stage (primarily didactic delivery). The design challenges of this constraint are shown in Table 11.1.

The 'Sage on the Stage' Constraint

One or a few speakers to fill the session (maintaining high quality performance); primary audience mode is listening (limited interaction); high potential for disengagement (disengaged audience). The design challenges of this constraint are shown in Table 11.2.

Table 11.1 Design challenges of the amphitheatre constraint

Design challenges	Possible playful solutions
Limited movement	Techniques to break up the space, e.g. create teams by splitting the theatre in half/sections and give them challenges; randomly select members of the audience as volunteers or to speak by throwing a beachball or other soft object; add cards or envelopes on (or under) seats or desks before the session, containing or linking to particular challenges or activities.
Enforced groupings	Pass something along long rows or around tables: Chinese whispers, an emerging collaborative narrative, pass Play-Doh or LEGO along to develop a model or prototype, etc.
	Build in movement: get people to swap tables or switch row ends when a bell sounds, to keep groups fluid and creative.
Didactic delivery	See 'Sage on the Stage' constraint.

Table 11.2 Design challenges of the 'sage on the stage' constraint

Design challenges	Possible playful solutions
Maintaining high-quality performance	Think about the session as a series of activities interspersed with presentation (see the 'Amphitheatre Constraint' for activity ideas).
	Use the space on the stage for props, acting, drawing giant cartoons, etc. to break up and vary the delivery.
Limited interaction	Break the division between speaker and audience:
Disengaged audience	reverse the view and get the audience to project back by standing up, shouting out, etc.; build in voting or opinion sourcing by getting attendees to stand/sit, hold cards up, etc.
	Start an argument on a key topic and invite members of the audience to argue against you: if you get beaten, award a prize.
	Bring people from the audience onto the stage to act things out or complete a challenge; use the audience as a map or board on which to create models (ask different people to stand up or use their hands to create points in the model/map).

The Constraint of Personal Permission

Context of the event: participants and/or sponsors are anticipating a serious programme (expectation of seriousness), so the presenter opts to play safe and deliver a traditional presentation (playing safe). The design challenges of this constraint are shown in Table 11.3.

Table 11.3 Design challenges of the personal permission constraint

Design challenges	Possible playful solutions
Expectation of 'seriousness' – participant	Give permission by offering an invitation to become playful: ask the audience to make hats, to throw a ball around or to pretend to sleep while still watching you. Build confidence: ask for the silliest or most impossible questions and then see if anyone else can answer them before you do. Bringing audience members onto the stage for a creative challenge to reduce the formality of the occasion.
Expectation of 'seriousness' – sponsor	Frame the playful approach in a critically acceptable value e.g. openness, ability to critique, creativity, innovation.
Playing safe – presenter	Start simple, e.g. playful icebreaker or interlude between more traditional talk. Plant a secret helper in the audience to ensure you get an initial response. Lecture theatre as magic circle: create a safe space where any question/comment is allowed, however simple, silly orstupid.

The Constraint of Slides

The dominance of a traditional 'talk to slides' approach, with text-heavy or endless bulleted lists, and slides that rarely change from talk to talk (inflexibility or, through lack of confidence or to avoid accessibility issues: risk aversion). Fixed video capture and/or podium in the theatre, causing presenter to stand in one spot (standing still). An imposed slide design or format, e.g. PechaKucha, limited number of slides, accessibility requirements, etc. (format restriction). The design challenges of this constraint are shown in Table 11.4.

The Constraint of Focus

The need to switch technology off and to have a single channel rather than multiple (absolute concentration). Risk of a back channel going off-message (risk management). Multiple media streams difficult to respond to (multiplicity of inputs). The design challenges of this constraint are shown in Table 11.5.

Practical Constraints

Limited time available to prepare presentation or to present it (time); problems when accessing the space to set up or dismantle activities or being given an inappropriate space (logistics); problems and failures during the presentation, such as technical issues, poor attendance or engagement (the unexpected). The design challenges of this constraint are shown in Table 11.6.

Table 11.4 Design challenges of the slides constraint

Design challenges	Possible playful solutions
Inflexibility	Choose your own adventure – the audience deciding the show by choosing the order of the slides either by vote or by random dice roll (see Case Study 28). Use simple slides (one word, one picture) and challenge the audience (or yourself) to create the subject around it.
Standing still	Use a GoPro and take the camera with you for a 'teachers' eye view' as you move around the theatre. Split the theatre into teams and walk up and down the walkways as you give the teams instructions or ask for their votes/responses.
Format restriction	Use the restriction as a design constraint: try to push it to its limits or work creatively to meet it playfully (e.g. maximum five slides? Ditch slides and bring nine props with you).
Risk aversion	Work playfully within constraints, as above. Flipped learning: ask your audience to be creative before the session and then use the session to share, discuss, vote on and reward their outputs.

Table 11.5 Design challenges of the focus constraint

Design challenges	Possible playful solutions
Absolute concentration – participants	Build in games or challenges at certain points to check understanding or crowdsource opinions. Embrace distractions – e.g. a playful activity driven through Twitter.
Risk management	Publicly show the back channel and ask for jokes, haikus or limericks to describe the content of the talk (to focus attention and subject playfully).
Multiplicity of inputs	Get additional help from a colleague or from the audience, e.g. choose the worst, funniest, weirdest comment or question every five minutes or at key points. Randomise access to particular channels, e.g. look at comments at particular times.

Table 11.6 Design challenges of the practical constraints

Design challenges	Possible playful solutions
Time	Get the audience to design the playful interactions, crowdsource ideas from other playful presenters – reward the best ideas. Have a 'core' presentation and optional extras, let the audience shape the presentation.
Logistics	Get the audience or helpers to assist you in set-up and dismantle, make this into a playful activity using competition or rewards.
The unexpected	Have other activities available and be prepared to change. Embrace the failure and make it fun or a challenge for the audience themselves.

Case Study 29: Interactive Keynote (Nicola Whitton/ Alex Moseley)

This one-hour interactive lecture was delivered at the LILAC Conference in 2016. As the opening session of the conference, it aimed to energise delegates and give them a taste of the different forms and potentials of playful learning.

The presentation was broken down into six different challenges that mapped onto six different motivational aspects of games identified in previous research. Each challenge was a mini-version of a game or playful activity that had successfully worked previously. Some involved all participants in the room, and some just a few. The challenges were:

1 **Collection.** Using an example of postcards collected by solving puzzles, a cypher puzzle was displayed to all delegates. The first person to tweet the answer was the winner.
2 **Creativity.** Demonstrating the potential for creativity problem-solving, audience members volunteered to join one of four small groups and were given the task of finding the most interesting thing they all had in common. Most interesting (as voted for by the audience) won.
3 **Collaboration.** To show the possibilities of escape rooms, a locked box was presented to the audience, which had to be solved together, starting by finding the real key among the hundreds of red herrings that had been hidden throughout the lecture theatre.
4 **Puzzle-solving.** The whole audience were asked to solve a puzzle and stand up in the correct formation to display the 'Y' or 'N' answer.
5 **Competition.** Delegates volunteered to be part of two teams, each team being cheered on by one half of the auditorium. Each team then had to complete a series of quick challenges as fast as possible
6 **Narrative.** To show the potential of immersive storytelling to provide context for learning, the audience had to engage with a number of fictional web and social media sites to solve a mystery and find a phone number (one of the presenter's phones) to call to submit their solution.

While the majority of people in the audience were highly engaged with the keynote, there were a few people who were clearly out of their comfort zones; this was perhaps a bridge too far from the traditional lecture format for some.

Designing with Constraints

Our first advice would be to start small, with the most obvious/appropriate/easy constraint, rather than trying to cover everything at once. Once you have identified a constraint/design challenge from the tables, use that to create your design brief. You can then use whatever design methodology you feel most comfortable or familiar with: in particular, we recommend co-design with a group of interested parties – e.g. an events team, or a selection of the intended audience. Involving more people leads to a greater number of creative design responses, from which you can select the best option (based on simplicity, creativity, playfulness and meeting the design brief), and ensures that you make the play accessible to a broader range of participants.

Once you have designed a creative approach on paper, it is important to 'playtest' or run through the design with real people, in an approximation of the live event. If you involved a team in co-design, you have a ready-made test group; otherwise, find a set of willing friends or colleagues who can help you test the approach. You might also, though, view the first live run of your activity as a further 'playtest': by viewing it in this way, you will find it easier to cope with anything that doesn't go to plan and can respond playfully by changing some aspects of the activity to work better with the audience and context you find yourself in (including deciding when to stop an activity or to remove an element you feel might not work).

Setting Up/Preparation

A playful presentation can often take more effort to set up. Playful interactions can take a wide variety of forms as suggested in the tables, for instance they may be invoked by the presenter, they could be virtually triggered through something like Twitter or they could be prompted by the participants themselves responding to a puzzle. This can lead to an unpredictable session, and it is important to think about how to respond. Identifying which content is critical to a session and which can either be flexed, adapted or even discarded is useful to this style of presenting. Setting critical timing points within the lecture is a useful mechanism which can be achieved through planning and a few practice run throughs, much as would be expected ahead of a keynote delivery.

The presentation itself may require more set-up: furniture, lighting, audio-visuals, projectors and any props or artefacts you need for your activities. Finding a friendly participant for both set-up and to help with the unexpected can be helpful.

There are opportunities to mitigate risks that may arise during the lecture. According to the nature of the presentation, audience behaviour can change. It can feel like permission has been given to disrupt or subvert in some cases, and this can create a different atmosphere than a speaker is used to. However, once permission is given to behave in this way, there should be a method to take control back, and it is good to find playful mechanisms to control timings and order. For example, an unusual image or sound could appear; a large soft object could be thrown into the audience; the speaker could put on a large hat. These *bounding activities* are important and can train the audience as indicators that activity is about to change.

Mitigating Risks

Risk, and mitigation thereof, has increased in importance in many sectors: certainly in business, and now in many education and community sectors too – with a focus on ensuring minimum liability for a company or organisation and to reduce the chance of anything affecting normal (or high) performance.

The playful suggestions we provided against the identified constraints A–G are clearly risks by the above definition: by deviating from a 'normal' didactic slide presentation, the speaker is opening themselves up to the chance of failure, or of unexpected outcomes for the session and for the participants. We might argue that, on the reverse side, there is a significant risk of disengagement and boredom if the didactic slide presentation remains 'normal', but this is unlikely to be a view shared by managers, CEOs and funders.

But we can mitigate against serious risk by keeping things simple to begin with (start small, build with confidence over time) and by playtesting approaches in a risk-free environment, such as with a group of work colleagues, students or friends, before running them in front of a genuine audience. By combining these two approaches, you will reduce risk to a minimum and increase the likelihood that you will be able to report positive outcomes (as simple, well-tested approaches are likely to work well in the final setting). Building a toolkit of playful approaches for starting and stopping activities, or for using with bored or over-active audiences, can also help to build resilience and therefore minimise risk over time.

There are other, smaller and more practical, risks involved in playful and creative presenting. The most common ones are:

- That there is no or little take-up of your activities.
- That the audience are so immersed in your activity that you cannot bring them back to the presentation.
- That, no matter how much you've tested it, a key prop or piece of tech fails to work.

The first two risks can be mitigated by thinking about the bounding of any activity: work out how to introduce it to the audience with an easy and attractive invitation to participate; set a defined time for it and share that with the audience (giving time updates and warnings as the end nears); and build in some space in your presentation timings to allow for one or two of your activities/talks to overrun slightly. You can also prepare tricks or devices to regain attention: such as a hooter/bell or a short audio or video clip to introduce the next section.

The third risk is an ever-present danger, but – as every experienced presenter knows – the easy answer is to always prepare a back-up for any tech or materials, regardless of how low their likelihood of failure. Where possible, have a second technology (e.g. different voting platform) available as backup; and – even better – have a physical (paper/prop/object) back-up to cover any wider tech failure.

Case Study 30: Playful Keynote (Rosie Jones)

This approach was used at the inaugural Playful Learning Conference with an audience of approximately 100 delegates, all engaged with playful learning, mainly from educational contexts. This session aimed to provide delegates with an understanding of the issues facing workplace play, demonstrate the possibilities of play and games in the workplace, understand how the environment can help support playful behaviours and enable people to participate in some simple playful activities that they could apply into practice.

A keynote was delivered that explored how play can support leaders and managers to develop creative and innovative environments, helping promote and inspire a culture that embraces change. All participants were given one of four team stickers on entrance to the lecture theatre. Playful activities were interspersed throughout the presentation; these were delivered through pre-scheduled tweets sent by GLNOIG (Games and Learning No Interest Group), who aimed to sabotage the session. These were scheduled to coincide with slides that delivered the activity, and this worked extremely well, even at times appearing to interact with delegates through some disparaging comments.

Players attempted to defeat GLNOIG by answering his four challenges, and points were assigned to teams. The four activities were:

Challenge 1. Weaken evil anti-play with a better meaning for GLNOIG; players had to devise and tweet their own funny anagrams.
Challenge 2. Tell me the answers to bouncing ball questions on Twitter; questions were written on a giant inflatable ball which was thrown around the room and questions answered by the catcher.
Challenge 3. Paper hats; delegates had to make their own origami hats and tweet themselves wearing them.

Challenge 4. Go to tap count (a website that simply counts the number of times the screen is tapped in a certain time); players had to attempt to get a high score.

While the session was highly interactive, the noise, excitement and disruption were quite distracting for the keynote to keep on track and to restore order when they wanted to be listened to.

Figure 11.1 Inflatable ball used in the playful keynote.
Credit: Playful Learning Conference by Mark Power.

An Example

Case Study 30 shows the practical application of play within a conference keynote. It can be argued that the occasion or personal permission as constraint was not present, and this might have been an easier task than 'traditional' keynotes, as it was at the Playful Learning conference where the invitation to play had already been given. However, this also increased the pressure of ensuring activities met the expectation of an already 'expert' audience. The preparation for this session was key and involved scheduled tweets, props and handouts. There was much that could go wrong, so friendly audience members were brought on board to assist should anything start to fail.

It would have been easy to become the 'sage on the stage' or to be constrained by slides, but playful solutions from the 'sage on the state' and 'personal permission' constraints were adopted. The audience were encouraged to shout out, ask questions and they made and wore hats. While the main talk was delivered from the front, a narrative developed on Twitter through an evil presence. This involved a number of practice runs to ensure timing of tweets worked with 'challenges' being set. By chance, the pre-written tweets ended up also helping with audience control, which at times became quite loud and chaotic (slides constraints); one tweet from the evil character silenced the crowd at the most appropriate moment. The 'amphitheatre' constraint also set a number of design challenges. There was very little room for movement, so techniques to break up the space were introduced. Audience members were put into teams using stickers on arrival, an inflatable ball was thrown at audience members to answer questions, origami hats were made and technology was used for competitive games.

For the keynote, this was a fun experience, but it easily could have become overwhelming. Much was out of the presenter's (and the organisers') control, the audience behaviour was very different to a traditional setting, activities were messy, inflatable balls hit participants and the timing was hard to judge. The playful solutions from practical constraints were certainly needed, and the presentation responded and flexed to the event to cope with the unexpected.

Conclusion

We believe that the constrained nature of formal presentations and the opportunities afforded by the theatre-like space provide an opportunity for playful design against those constraints. The resulting playful presentations are more interactive for the audience and provide feedback and lessen the need for continual high-quality content for the presenter. We hope that you are able to utilise the constraints we have detailed as design briefs to introduce some form of playful interaction into your presentations. Start small but think carefully and playfully about using the space or the occasion as an opportunity: be both creative and inventive. With more and wider experimentation of playful presentation forms, we hope that this can become the 'traditional' and replace the expected yet ultimately lacking 'sage on the stage'.

12 Playful Tools and Technologies

Katie Piatt

Introduction

Digital technologies and physical artefacts can be used to support play in many ways. From simple dice, stickers or marbles through to bespoke developed apps and video games, there is a growing range of tools and technologies available, effective in an equally diverse range of learning activities. This chapter discusses examples of tools and technologies used previously to facilitate play and describes what worked well to meet different needs at learning events. The chapter focusses particularly on tools and technologies to facilitate three different aspects of play: competition, collaboration and creativity.

When designing or planning a playful learning activity, you need to be clear on what you want the activity to achieve and can then select tools or technologies to support it. It can be useful to draw on the ten steps of game design model provided by Moseley and Whitton (Moseley & Whitton, 2015), summarised in Figure 12.1. Although this model is based on educational game design, it could actually be applied to the design of any playful learning activity. The first phase starts by thinking about the context in which the activity will be used, defining the learning objectives you want it to address and identifying the constraints. When considering tools and technologies, this might particularly relate to accessibility, availability, cost and considerations around technology such as compatibility, usability and acceptability by participants.

From the model, the next phase focusses on the main design where you determine the type of activity and core mechanics; this is where you can choose the tools and technologies you will make use of. A prototype of the activity can be created and tested. Once the main model is in place, the model brings in narratives and dynamics to consider the roles of the players and add colour and interest to the game, including elements of risk, sabotage opportunities and developed rules. Finally, the model reviews the activity against the original learning outcomes to ensure that they are being met by the final design (it is easy to move off-course when enthused with a playful design project). This model is a useful starting point as a sense check and consideration what (and whether) technologies and physical tools are needed as part of a playful activity.

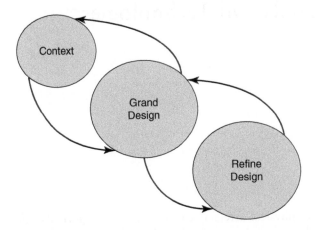

Figure 12.1 Three phases of the 10-step model of game design. (Moseley & Whitton, 2015).

Should You Use Technology?

It is tempting to look to technology for solutions, and indeed the affordances of technology provide a range of abilities for you to use in your playful design. However, it is important to harness technology into your designed activity because of what it can do for your design, identified by Salen and Zimmerman (2004) as four primary abilities: to offer immediate, interactive feedback; to store and manipulate information easily; to automate complicated procedures; and to facilitate communication between players.

Case Study 31: Murder at ECEL (Katie Piatt)

A conference game to demonstrate game-based learning at the European Conference on eLearning held at the University of Brighton in 2011 for 200 international delegates. The game took the form of a whodunit murder mystery, which was to be solved during the conference, through clues and a website to track progress. The clues required engagement with online learning activities to provide a practical demonstration of game-based learning.

A whodunit scenario was chosen as the game design, as it was a mystery format that an international audience could all identify with. There were six activities in all: three that could be completed online using existing websites, and three that required engagement with somebody at the conference. An example of an online clue:

What's the name of the swab used to collect DNA samples from cheek cells?

Link: http://forensics.rice.edu/ (Rookie Training, Forensic Biology)

The three clues at the conference were all accessible without puzzle-solving expertise, which meant that we did not lose players by trying to be overly cryptic (a danger when experienced puzzlers set clues for novices). For example, an easy 'poster' clue required them to spot that one of the posters on display was by Professor #Brown; it was of four elephants, with 'elephant' being the answer they needed to enter on the website. The six clues led the players to six numbers, which together formed a phone number. Once dialled, this rang a phone planted on one of the conference organisers, who was happy to act appropriately when his phone rang revealing him as the murderer! With a captive audience interested in e-learning, we had relatively high participation: 41 participants out of 200 for the first online clue, then descending down to 11 people who eventually completed all tasks.

An example of the ability of technology to easily store and manipulate information is shown in Case Study 31. The website in the game was a basic html form to check players' responses, and everything entered was logged to a text file. This was a simple technical solution to set up, but it gave us a very clear idea of how players were progressing and allowed us to assess take-up throughout the day.

As Sicart (2014) says, "we don't need computing to play" (p. 99), but the things technology can do well can create an expanded world in which we can play. Making use of existing software can augment your playful activity and add an interactive element in a way that is not possible without doing so. However, using technology generally comes with risks, as technology keeps changing, usually outside our control. This may cause prohibitive problems and increase costs. You may also want to consider the level of your players' digital literacies and if indeed this is a way that they want to learn, as well as availability of devices to complete digital tasks.

Tools and Technologies in #SenateSecrets

I will now explore three kinds of activity you might want to create at your event – competition, collaboration and creativity – using the FOTE 2014 conference game #SenateSecrets as a case study throughout (Case Study 32).

The Future of Technology in Education Conference (FOTE) is an annual event hosted by the University of London Computer Centre, based in the historic Senate House, which is part of the University of London. With over 400 delegates, the conference serves as a platform to share creative and challenging ideas about the use of technology in education within the education community. FOTE often tries out new conference format ideas and has previously had games running through the conference (see Case Study 1, the 2012 case study). For the 2014 conference, the Association for Learning Technology Games and Learning Special Interest Group were invited to use FOTE as an event to develop some playful ideas exemplifying the use of games for education.

Case Study 32: #SenateSecrets (Katie Piatt/Alex Moseley)

Building on the buzz around the 2012 conference game (see Case Study 1), the annual Future of Technology in Education (FOTE) conference commissioned a new game in 2014, which we designed as a treasure hunt that would take place online and offline before and during the conference. The game provided delegates a chance to explore the history of the venue, Senate House in London, both online and in the building itself during the conference through a series of puzzles and challenges.

A locked box with six padlocks (see Figure 12.2) was placed in a prominent position in the main area of the conference venue. Delegates could work individually and collaboratively to unlock these padlocks as the clues were released during the day to reveal the contents of the Senate Chest. The six clues were challenges designed to focus on aspects of the conference, such as networking or meeting the sponsors. Each of the six padlocks had an accompanying challenge, which were released throughout the day. Delegates worked together to unlock the box by undertaking challenges that focussed on aspects of the conference such as networking and meeting the sponsors.

The game was introduced at the start of the conference with the tale of the hidden treasure of Senate House, and challenges appeared throughout. For example:

- There was a key hidden under one of the chairs in the main auditorium, which was announced during the opening talk, causing all delegates to start looking under their chairs.
- Four different secret business cards were located across the exhibitors' tables. Finding all four and correctly arranging them led to a specific ventilation grille where a key was hidden.

- In groups of three, delegates passed the 'security guard' (an actor) to enter a room in which we had hidden the correct key and 20 red herring keys. Teams could only leave with one key at a time to select the right one to unlock the padlock.

During the afternoon coffee break, the final padlock was unlocked, revealing the treasure (sweets to share with all delegates). We concluded the narrative at the end of the conference with prizes for the padlock holders.

All delegates were aware of the game, and we estimate around 5–10% took an active part in unlocking padlocks, although noticeably larger numbers were heard discussing the game, and everyone was involved in searching beneath their seats for the hidden key during the opening launch. However, we failed to recognise that players are clever and will not necessarily unlock a padlock immediately just because they are holding a key. One player wanted to save her key to the end in order to unlock the final lock and risked destroying the flow of the game; we quickly adapted but had not anticipated this.

Figure 12.2 A mystery box with six padlocks.
Credit: Katie Piatt.

Following a brainstorming meeting and tour at the conference venue, the game team arrived at the idea of a game that provided examples of playful learning through a series of puzzles and challenges. The game would also provide delegates with a chance to explore the amazing history of Senate House both online and in the hallways of the building itself during the event. We aimed specifically to design three aspects of the game: competitive challenge, collaboration and creativity.

In the #SenateSecrets game, competition was created by delegates trying to be the first to complete each of the six challenges in order to locate the key to the next padlock. In an early challenge, a key was hidden under one of the chairs in the main lecture venue, which was announced during the opening remarks. This caused all delegates to start furiously looking under their chairs, heightening excitement and competition in the room. This element also provided an unexpected element, which Schell (2008) describes as the lens of surprise; the delegates were not expecting to suddenly find they might be sitting on a key. Collaboration opportunities were provided to the delegates through challenges requiring finding other people or speaking to others. For example, one challenge required delegates to visit the exhibitors at the conference. Four different business cards were located across the exhibitors' tables. Speaking to the exhibitors would result in being awarded a card, then finding all four and correctly arranging them led delegates to a specific location where a key was hidden. Another challenged required delegates to meet each other. In groups of three, they had to pass a 'security guard' (actually a member of the design team in fancy dress) to enter a room containing a real key and a large number of red herring keys. Teams could only leave with one key at a time to select the right one, requiring some discussion and planning. Creative opportunities were provided to the delegates through challenges that involved taking photos, videos and puzzle-solving challenges.

One challenge asked delegates to look out for photo clues on the conference Twitter account throughout the day and then explore the venue to find where the photo was taken, which enabled them to locate the missing digits from our photos to discover the combination of a padlock. The final challenge of the event involved a puzzle-based escape-room-like activity. Players returned to the room they had visited earlier to spot that some books had appeared and had to then work out that there was a code to be revealed with an ultraviolet light on the spines of these books.

Case Study 33: Playful Away Day (Rosie Jones)

A variety of playful techniques and approaches were used at an off-site away day with approximately 70 library-related staff with a broad range of roles from the library of a large university. The day aimed to offer opportunities for the whole library to network and build teams and introduce a playful culture to encourage innovation and creativity.

The day presented a series of playful activities as well as introducing some of the theory behind the use of play in academia. These activities included:

- Giving the delegates the opportunity to create and 'pimp' their own name badges.

- A keynote speaker who was an expert in play to add credibility.
- 'Wreck it' creativity journals (containing a variety of disruptive tasks and thinking activities) being passed around throughout the day.
- Using game creation as an approach to solve an issue or teach a complicated topic.
- Challenge cards used throughout the day to encourage positive behaviour e.g. offering a hugging service for an hour for anyone that needed it.

This was all led by the director, and this worked well for giving the team permission to be playful at work.

Playful Tools and Technologies

The #SenateSecrets case study shows how different tools and technologies can be combined to create a playful conference game underpinned with competitive challenge, collaboration and creative tasks. This section describes some alternative ideas for ways in which digital and physical artefacts can be used to create competitive challenges, foster collaboration or provide a creative stimulus.

Competitive Challenge

Challenging delegates to compete with others can be an effective motivation for some people. In the business world, competition is high, and replicating that at an event between delegates or in teams can be effective. Beyond this case study, other methods of creating challenge might be:

- **Use of a scoreboard or leaderboard.** This may be a tool like Rise.global (www.rise.global), which automatically tracks tweets, or just a spreadsheet or handwritten whiteboard. Leaderboards are effective at longer-running events that take place over several days and provide a way of sustaining engagement. Leaderboards are also effective for dispersed participants, such as a departmental online quiz.
- **Use of a quiz tool.** Kahoot, as an example of a free online quiz tool, is great for classroom settings to add a sense of competition while testing learners' knowledge or gathering their opinions.
- **Use of a location-based tool.** Actionbound is an example of an app that can be used to create treasure hunt style activities for learners, encouraging players to explore a physical space against the clock. From my experience, I would suggest that where players are working with an app on a shared device, teams of two are optimal, as one can focus on the app while the other can look for clues/destinations.

- **Use of random choice tools.** There are a range of free 'spin-the-wheel' online tools, which are great for classroom activities to quickly add a chance or randomisation element and allow learners to select the options and then spin. Physical dice or a deck of playing cards are also simple ways of providing random elements in small co-located groups.

Collaboration

Providing learners with opportunities to collaborate allows experiences to be shared, networking to happen and brings all the benefits of group working. Beyond the case study given, other methods of creating collaboration might be:

- **Use of social media.** Playful events often generate a good deal of social media activity, particularly on platforms such as Twitter. Common social platforms help connect online learners and widen the reach of an event. If your event is likely to use social media, then give some thought to hashtags, ideally making use of the main conference hashtag to integrate your activity into the main event. Sicart (2014) provides interesting examples, such as using Twitter bots for performative playful processes. You might also consider asking learners to create social media accounts with an avatar to provide them a difference voice for your event (see Case Study 11).
- **Use of collectable artefacts.** A mechanism such as collecting, comparing or trading sets of cards is a good way of encouraging players to interact, while also appealing to human instinct to create sets. This can make a good icebreaker activity (see Case Studies 2 and 17). Collecting stickers for achievements, displayed on an event lanyard, is another good way of encouraging learners to talk and share their own experiences. Cards can be cheaply produced by adding stickers to blank playing cards (available online) or ordering custom printed cards from companies such as Moo.
- **Use of focal points.** A centrally located item such as a large locked box can add a reason for learners to congregate in one place in a venue and network (as in Case Study 32).
- **Use of escape rooms techniques.** Escape rooms use a variety of collaborative puzzles in a locked room scenario to force players to work together to solve puzzles. This is often used as a good team building activity as a whole (see Case Studies 22 and 23), but elements of escape rooms (e.g. locked boxes, padlock codes, hidden ultraviolet messages) can be used on their own to create interest and encourage people to work with one another.
- **Use of collaborative writing.** Stories or poems can be co-created using paper-folding techniques passed around a group (hiding previous

writing and then revealing all at the end), or use of websites such as Storium or Storyjacker. A shared sense of ownership adds value to the resulting writing.

Creativity

Creative activities give learners an opportunity to explore alternate possibilities and choose their own directions. If players are given the chance to use their imaginations, they can consider new ways of being in the world. Beyond this case study, other methods of creating creative opportunities might be:

- **Use of online creativity tools.** For example, Padlet is a great resource for workshop/classroom activities where learners can create content and easily share online with each other. A shared drawing area, such as use of annotation tools in Google Hangouts or other webinar software, is another way of allowing learners to express themselves (even if they are just adding moustaches to photos!).
- **Use of photos.** Asking participants to take selfies or photos with certain constraints works well at exhibitions to engage people, which can then be shared on social media to promote the event. This can be combined with dressing up, cardboard speech bubbles, giant photo frames, etc. Displaying the results on large screens also helps share the creative output.
- **Opportunities for gaming.** Players like to use their creativity to 'game' the activity and see if they can beat the system. This can be a problem, such as the example above, where the holder of the key decided to hold onto it until the end and not unlock the padlock, but if anticipated, this could be used to great advantage and praised, for example preparing a 'sneakiest player' award with extra benefits or sanctions.
- **Use of creative materials.** LEGO, colouring pens, scissors and cardboard and Play-Doh all give learners the chance to create something new to express their ideas (see Case Study 36). At an event, providing a selection of materials in a central location can be an opportunity to co-construct a large exhibit, an example being a multi-person-generated marble run at the Playful Learning Conference (see Figure 12.3).
- **Use of technology.** Access to technology, such as a Raspberry Pi or Makey Makey, gives learners opportunities to get creative with real-world interfaces. Examples include a musical piano on venue steps using security pressure pads connected to an Arduino, or a hand-clap controller for exploring Google Earth. Access to devices such as iPads provides scope for creating stop-frame videos or 360-degree photos – all of which are great outlets for creativity in learners and produce easily shareable outputs.

Figure 12.3 Building a marble run at Playful Learning.
Credit: Playful Learning Conference by Mark Power.

Conclusion

The in-depth case study described in this chapter, #SenateSecrets, was selected for the range of activities it included, resulting in high visibility of the game and good external reach. In terms of engagement, all delegates at the conference were aware of the game through pre-advertising, mentions during the opening remarks and stickers on the registration desk. Large numbers were heard discussing the game during coffee breaks, and the hidden key challenge engaged almost the whole lecture theatre in searching beneath their seats.

Of course, a game that makes use of several different tools and technologies does require meticulous planning. To summarise the lessons and tips I've learned, as advice when planning your own event:

1   Start simple and build up elements of your event activity. Although it may seem too complex to use such a wide range of mechanisms, individual elements (such as a trivia quiz, padlocks, etc.) can and should be tested before everything is pulled together.
2   A physical artefact (such as the padlocked box) provides a good focus point for a game with a lot of elements, especially when there is surprise involved (such as the contents, to be revealed!).
3   Do not worry if you cannot track player numbers and other metrics. At a conference, many delegates are just happy that there *is* a game but do not necessarily want to take part. Try to include one or two 'mass' activities in opening sessions to alert everyone to the game.
4   Players unsuccessful engaging with one element tend not to continue with your activity even if elements are distinct and unrelated.

Build player confidence by choosing early activities that everyone can easily complete.

5 Include physical spaces to explore and real people (such as a security guard) to add live elements (for example, a 'locked room puzzle' element, which could create a buzz at an event).

As always, it is important to work out what you want your event to achieve and then to select the right tools and technologies to achieve your aims. I hope that the ideas presented here have given you ideas with which to integrate technology and tools playfully into your own events.

13 Playful Evaluation

Mark Langan

Introduction

Customer feedback pervades the modern age. To some an annoying curse; to others a valuable form of communication that gets things aired and changed, or maybe a useful collection of insights into a particular product sold online. Whatever their views, most people are probably aware of being asked frequently for ratings, views and general feedback. Events such as conferences are a prime candidate for asking participants about views of their experiences, and a good conference feedback system needs to get delegates to respond in order to gather meaningful information, and then interpret and use the outcomes appropriately. Each step has its challenges, but in particular the first stage of enticing participants to respond could be suited ideally to the use of playful approaches.

The methods for the collection, processing and communication of peoples' views can be a very serious (and big) business. The use of self-responding survey outcomes can be of significant value, but there is always the possibility that they may overly influence opinions. Customer enquiry based on evaluative feedback tends to assume that the outputs are valid and of high quality, but this is often not the case (Maniaci & Rogge, 2014).

Of course, instruments and techniques used for participant evaluations will all have their own strengths and weaknesses. Participant surveys are prevalent in many forms, usually as rapid tools to administer and complete in either digital or physical forms. A common feature of modern events is the 'smile sheet' provided when those who have attended events are preparing to leave. The ubiquitous nature of such rapid surveys has put them under scrutiny and they have been widely criticised. Many factors can influence survey outcomes that are extrinsic to the survey itself, and also the type of survey and the mode in which it is delivered can be critical to its validity. Respondents generally want to provide socially desirable responses; 'acquiescence bias' and 'survey fatigue' occur due to the requests to complete many, overly-long surveys; recent experiences of completing surveys influence respondents; and sample bias can lead to unrepresentative views (for example when respondents are self-selecting).

Podsakoff and colleagues (2003) overviewed many of these potential biases in behavioural research, many of which are pertinent to survey design. They highlight how participant responses to survey items are influenced by the wording of the questions or statements (e.g. positive statements tend to lead to ratings of higher satisfaction) and the influence of the time and environment in which evaluations take place (e.g. affecting their mood or personal agenda). There is also the consideration of how those administering the surveys might (unduly) influence participant responses through their actions. Many organisers of events want to show that their venture was a success and may have to officially report on their feedback (including any accompanying metrics). This can lead to an intrinsic desire to get positive feedback, something that can result in a biased view being reported. Adding more playful and fun mechanisms to participant feedback is a decision that may be interpreted (by some) as a means to elicit more positive responses. It is important to consider how this might be viewed, and any potential biases, before investing in developing more creative participant feedback approaches. This reflection should acknowledge perspectives of your participants, scrutineers and any other stakeholders who might get the wrong end of the stick.

Case Study 34: Build Your Feedback … (Andrew Walsh)

This activity has been used in higher education institutions and in wider training for many groups but suits any context where you want to gather information about the user experience. It aims to use metaphors to allow people to talk about issues or learning in a safe way. I've used similar approaches to this to gain feedback about a service or building and at the end of training events. It can be adapted to suit the training event, so for example, using LEGO in a similar way at the end of a LEGO training session.

This approach asks participants to build or otherwise create something as a metaphor for their feedback.

So typical questions to them might be:

1   Draw a sketch showing what you learnt today.
2   Choose an object (chosen from a selection of random objects) that represents what you'll do differently after today's event.
3   Build a model of your ideal conference.

Participants are then asked to talk about what they have created. It does not matter what their 'creation' looks like, as it is there primarily to give them permission to talk about the object, rather than feeling they are talking about the issue directly. It also helps people reflect on the issues you want through thinking with their hands as they create something to discuss with you. It can be quite difficult for some people to do an exercise like this, especially if they feel that they are not artistic or if they struggle to think in terms of metaphors rather than in literal terms. It helps if participants have been doing creative exercises beforehand, so it suits more creative workshops much better than something closer to a lecture style.

Event Performance Evaluation

This chapter considers ways to get feedback from events that are more playful in approach. However, let us first briefly consider the wider literature base, including consideration of the financial dimensions. There is significant literature about how participant feedback can be part of a process to measure 'return on investment' (ROI) or claims of views on documenting benefits, such as what the participants gain in terms of enhancements of learning organizations, communities of practice and knowledge construction (see, for example, Phillips, Breining, & Phillips, 2008; Wiessner, Hatcher, Chapman, & Storberg-Walker, 2008). There are also many texts that consider the role of performance evaluation from a project/event manager's perspective (e.g. Tum, Norton, & Wright, 2006). In this chapter I will not explore impact assessments or evaluations for the purposes of 'pure research', or consider primarily financially-driven approaches. These concepts appear most important for publicly funded initiatives. This chapter will focus on 'event evaluation'.

Types of Event Feedback

It is easy to follow the herd and use smile sheets at the end of an event, providing happily satiated 'customers' with a sample of rather standard-looking questions or statements to be hurriedly 'ticked and returned'. The evaluator distributes them on paper (or online), participants fill them in, they collect (or download) the returns, read them, record a few things and probably report some quantitative and qualitative outcomes. It is likely that they would like to see very positive feedback (perhaps capturing a few choice quotes for future reporting), confirming what they did was more than acceptable and would perhaps agree with some of the more constructive/ negative comments to enhance future events. For those that want to stick to this type of approach but also do something a little different, consider altering: the mode of delivery, the types of enquiry or the feel/environment of the feedback process. As a means to begin the process of changing your existing practices, I will first consider some of the 'classic' approaches to collecting participant feedback (see Table 13.1). The simplistic split between typologies as 'ratings' and 'comments' is artificial, and often ratings and open comments are combined in surveys. Some variants have been omitted that do not easily sit within this structure, for example telephone and online conference calls.

This overview of basic methods for gathering participant feedback is not exhaustive but covers the main areas in use. The suggestions are categorised as digital or physical, although I acknowledge there are many ways to categorise techniques like these and that all these examples are open to variability in the basic approaches used. For example, methods that require the participants to be present ('in the moment') have strengths and weaknesses compared to asynchronous approaches. Technological solutions may be commercial packages designed for this purpose, use social media or on-screen response systems.

There is a wide variety of technology available for event feedback through bespoke software and apps, social media and real-time response systems. The choice of technology to enable feedback systems will need to consider available devices, for example whether participants should use their own smartphones, bespoke devices (such as voting pods or 'clickers') or in-house tablets. The costs and management of the systems may dictate preferences. There also should be some consideration about what happens if technology fails (is there a physical or different digital backup?). Inclusivity is also important, for example, for participants who are visually impaired or unable to use certain technologies; thinking through barriers to inclusivity and alternative methods is key.

The wording of anything asked of participants, such as survey items (and their order), will vary depending on what it is you want to find out. These may be limited by media choices in length and form, and designers need to consider whether they want numerical (e.g. ratings, or levels of agreement to statements) or textual outcomes, or both. They also need to consider how long participants will engage with the particular mode of feedback.

Table 13.1 Basic methods for collecting participant feedback at events

Type	Form	
	Physical	*Digital*
Ratings	'Smile sheets', ratings Paper questionnaires Face-to-face survey Voting slips/chips	Online survey ratings Real time, on-screen ratings
Open comments	Interviews, focus groups Post boxes Participant journals	Social media Real-time, on-screen comments Comment boxes (e.g. website) Emails

Face-to-face approaches can lead to very detailed discussions, and the problem of acquiring and analysing data from meetings, focus groups and interviews can be costly and daunting.

Qualitative Versus Quantitative Feedback

In general, event participant feedback is collected in a rapid and simple way, as it is not intended for in-depth research purposes. A common way to elicit comments is to keep the invitation to comment very open, for example just asking for 'any comments' or creating the positive/negative division by asking for views on 'the best things' and 'areas to improve'. Note the positive orientation of the latter statement, which avoided asking about the 'worst things'. This is commonplace and is one of the factors that contributes to the skewed nature of customer feedback, where the majority of customer satisfaction surveys tend towards the positive (Peterson & Wilson, 1992). Open comments can be organised into themes and subthemes, by approaches such as thematic analysis and survey comments have been shown to at least broadly relate to accompanying ratings; for example, better experiences receive better ratings, although specific aspects of the experience may have greater influence than others on overall satisfaction (Langan et al., 2017).

Survey ratings, like smile sheets, are necessarily closed designs, as they should clearly identify what is being requested of the participant and provide some form of scale to record responses. Five-point Likert-type scales are very common, with ratings from 'strongly agree' to 'strongly disagree' and a neutral response in the middle. There are arguments about having a neutral response at all (Krosnick et al., 2002) or whether to have more options, for example a seven-point Likert scale has been suggested as more suitable for statistical analyses (Carifio & Perla, 2008). Open, written comments are a means to allow participants to report on a wider set of their thoughts rather than being constrained to respond in limited pre-set ways. If discursive in-depth, verbal feedback is required, some form of face-to-face approach may be appropriate.

Timing of Feedback

A great deal of feedback is acquired after an event has taken place (or is about to finish). However, there are opportunities to canvass opinions during the event or even earlier, when arranging events. For example, gathering feedback on the pre-event communications and planning. Often with events, the requirement is to gain information about its perceived success after the participants have experienced the events offerings. Here there is the question of either gathering views 'in the moment' (for example in a final session) or after the participants have departed. This timing can have significant influences on the responses.

Real-time feedback relies largely on human emotions within a particular situation, moderated by that person's particular views of the world. This is termed 'affective reasoning' and differs from 'reflective reasoning' that would take place after the event and is moderated by an individual's memory of past experiences. Of course, those 'after the event reflections' also happen in a particular moment, where the person's emotional responses are influencing their views and conclusions. It has long been known that if someone completes a survey when they are in a particularly good mood, it will likely be more positive than one completed in a bad mood (Schwarz & Clore, 1983).

When feedback is gathered after an event is over and the participants have departed, this is largely out of the control of those requesting the evaluation survey. It can be more difficult to get responses after participants have departed, which reduces sample sizes and potentially creates sample bias. The change in mode of survey, for example from written to online responses, can have significant impacts on the outcomes (Burton, Civitano, & Steiner-Grossman, 2012). The emotions of an event cannot be fully captured with post-event feedback, and potential advantages of real-time feedback include higher proportions of participants responding and the possibility of capturing the 'buzz' of the event within the respondents' feedback. Being with the participants 'in the moment' also offers opportunity for playfulness with the advantage of someone being there to contextualise and drive the activities that lead to feedback acquisition.

Case Study 35: The Feedbasket (James Charnock)

The 'Feedbasket' was the last activity of the final one-hour session at the end of the first two Playful Learning conferences, involving all participants that stayed until the end (around 80 people). The exercise took about ten minutes, with all attendees sat in a lecture theatre. The brief was to:

- Encourage attendees to reflect on their conference experience and provide useful feedback to the organising committee.
- Generate energy through a physical activity that is fun and achieve a full complement of responses.
- Obtain feedback that would both provide an evaluation of participant views of the value of the conference and also information to modify future events.

Participants completed a rapid, paper-based survey (six basic, open questions) of their views of the conference. They then modelled the paper into aeroplanes based on a design outlined on the back of the sheet (or screwed them up) to throw at the conference 'feedbasket' (a plastic bin in the first year and a basketball hoop in the second). The first to get it in was awarded a nominal prize, for others there was the fun and satisfaction of an accurate throw or hitting the organisers standing at the front. The term 'feedbasket' was well-received, and all participants provided feedback. There was a buzz as the participants left the room. It is possible that the process of reflection and writing was time-limited, and the participants wanted to throw their responses more than provide quality feedback.

Figure 13.1 Using the feedbasket to collect conference feedback.
Credit: Playful Learning Conference by Mark Power.

Playful Evaluation

Now that some of the main parameters of evaluation have been discussed, it is time to consider how to create a more playful event evaluation. First, identify the context and needs; the following questions are useful to consider:

- **Purpose.** What do you really want to know (e.g. were core services effective; is this an opportunity to gather feedback for enhancement or marketing)? What information do you have to provide to other stakeholders as evidence (e.g. overall satisfaction, response rate)? What will you do with the feedback (analyses, quotes, issues)? Do you want the process of acquiring participant feedback process to be a 'feature' of the event?

- **Process.** When do you want to gather feedback (e.g. expectations in advance, during the event at any point or continuously, after the event has finished)? Do you need to consider anonymization GDPR (e.g. storage and use of information from/to participants)? How can you maximise response (e.g. participant motivation)? How can the experience of giving feedback be a positive aspect of the event (e.g. influencing the environment, appropriateness of timing)? Do you want/ how can you encourage genuine, considered, balanced feedback (e.g. narrative around feedback)? Do you want to create a feedback system that favours positive feedback (e.g. positively worded survey items) or place focus on the areas to improve (e.g. a complaint letter)? How will you create an inclusive feedback system that is accessible to all your participants (e.g. accessibility of the methods of information acquisition)?
- **Playfulness.** How can you tailor your feedback mechanism to fit the personality of your event (e.g. level of seriousness, playful on a theme)? Do you want to gamify the feedback experience (e.g. leaderboards)? Do you want to be playful in acquiring feedback (e.g. active delivery)? Do you have a particular time/place to gather feedback in a playful fashion (e.g. a final 'wrap-up' session)?

The basic approaches to gathering feedback that I have described are likely to be familiar to many event organisers, partly through personal experiences of providing feedback. Due to the ubiquitous nature of customer feedback, I suggest that it is likely that more novel and fun methods are likely to be retained in the memory of participants. Indeed, I have found that feedback activities themselves can be used to add to the positive experience of an event. Playfulness can provide a counter to 'feedback fatigue' by surprising respondents and adding fun to the process. Among the most useful playful approaches (or lenses) for this purpose are: creativity, disruption, constraints and failure.

Creativity can be what links an event theme to an evaluation approach. Rather than defaulting to a standard email questionnaire or a smile sheet, use the theme as a platform for imaginative approaches. If there is a difficult and very formal theme, then there is a constraint, and that in itself can lead to a playful outcome (see constraints below). Within a creative theme there are numerous possibilities. For example, if an event deals with electronics or robotics, there could be a feedback sheet or platform where attendees link circuits together to connect components/phrases that describe their experiences, or maybe they write or pin comments onto a giant good robot or giant evil robot. Participants at an education-focussed event could be asked to 'graffiti' the white board at the front of the lecture hall as they leave the final session.

Disruption provides a useful platform for playfulness in feedback. This notion is often positioned (negatively) on the respondents' side as they respond to unwanted imposed evaluations, poorly designed evaluations or feedback fatigue. For an entertaining example of this practise, browse the customer feedback reviews of the otherwise innocuous "Box Canvas Print of Paul Ross" and "Three Wolf Moon T-shirt" on Amazon UK, where there are tales of how the products have transformed lives, led to divorce, solved world peace, etc. Typically, in student feedback surveys, or on political voting slips, there are many examples of 'spoiled' responses (e.g. witticisms, ironic statements). This disruptive approach to imposed systems has been described by Woodcock (2017) as 'socialism from below', where the imposed playfully disrupt the system by spoiling or interfering with set mechanisms. This disruptive approach can be used in the playful design of feedback methods. If the evaluation itself is disruptive to what respondents are expecting, then they might be more likely to find it interesting or worthwhile.

Constraints might appear to limit options: common constraints include stakeholder opinions, financial constraints and venue limitations. Many games use constraints to their advantage to create highly playful experiences, and this is also true of playful design. If a feedback sheet has to look 'normal', why not be playful with the wording or have a set of stickers fall out when a plain envelope is opened? If there is not time to collect feedback before everyone leaves, give them something interesting to do on their journey home. Maybe they have to take and 'tweet' a picture that sums up their conference experience. Use the constraint as a design parameter to allow participants to be creative rather than a problem to deal with.

Failure has been described earlier in this chapter in the context of event evaluation and is often geared at gaining positive feedback. Why not celebrate failure and invite attendees to join in celebrating it and learning from it? Have a 'naughty corner' on your feedback sheet; ask questions such as "I never want to see another _____ again!"; or as the library at the University of Kent asked their students, invite attendees to write a break-up (or love) letter to the conference. Use of techniques to celebrate should provide different perspectives in the feedback compared to more standard approaches.

Examples of Playful Evaluation

There are numerous ways to be playful and myriad themes that can be adopted as a means to drive playfulness in any given event. Here the theme provides the constraint to 'playfully work' within, and coming up with the ideas and means to be playful can be the most fun part of the event lifecycle.

To provide a framework to give some ideas and examples, I will use a basic pirate theme. Revisiting the basic methods of evaluation outlined previously (see Table 13.1), I have applied a pirate lens to each as an example of how to move into a playful arena (see Table 13.2). I acknowledge that

Table 13.2 Examples of playful methods for collecting participant feedback at events

Feedback mechanism	Playful development	Pirate-themed example
'Smile sheets', ratings	Replace smiles with icons linked to an event theme. Consider rewording items in language relevant to the event 'personality' or theme.	Survey ratings are symbolised by differing levels of pirate gold or numbers of parrots on a pirate's shoulders. Participants return as paper aeroplanes.
Paper questionnaires	Written in language suiting the theme. Distributed by organiser in costume, with appropriate music. Unusual vessel for collecting feedback.	Participants in arena screw up feedback sheets and throw them as cannon balls at an organiser who is dressed as a pirate. Prizes such as chocolate gold coins can be awarded for the best shot.
Face-to-face survey	Surveyors dressed in costume and in a booth linked to the theme. Perhaps playing a game as part of the survey in role play.	"How could we have improved your hunt for treasure, me hearty?" "So you're jumping ship, are you? What can we do to get you back for more adventures, shipmate?"
Voting slips/chips	The voting chips or slips, and the vote box, take on a playful theme.	'Pieces of eight' are dropped into one of three pirate treasure chests labelled 'Desert island (with rum)', 'Desert island (without rum)' and 'Davy Jones's Locker'.
Online survey ratings	Modifications to language, images relevant to theme.	Language and image modifications as above (e.g. superimposed pirate ship background).
Real-time, on-screen ratings	Modifications to language, images relevant to theme. Light-hearted compere.	Language and image modifications as above (e.g. superimposed pirate ship background).
Interviews, focus groups	Embedded into existing group activities with simplistic, themed, playful rewards.	Treasure hunt theme in groups that ends in a group discussion and prizes.
Post boxes	'Pimped' versions. Use of technology inside such as AI voice.	Post box is designed to look like a pirate treasure chest. Wording stresses value of their feedback (like treasure).
Participant journals	Themed, referred to during event (potentially on social media or gamified; see Case Study 11).	Pirate captain's log, succinctly accounting their event experiences and challenges faced.
Social media	Alter egos (see Case Study 11).	Pirate name generator and dressing up opportunity at star of conference for the photo. Media photo could also be pirate themed toys or drawings.
Real-time response systems	Modifications to language, images relevant to theme. Light-hearted compere.	Language and image modifications as above.
Emails		
Comment boxes (e.g. website)		

the success of any particular approach depends on the participants, the location, the professional purpose/theme of the event and the ambition of the team delivering the event (and feedback if these are separate systems).

Willingness to Play

Depending on the audience, the event experience, the location, the timing and even the food and weather at the time, respondents may not be in the mood to give feedback; let alone to be playful. Evaluators therefore have to think quite carefully about the 'invitation to play': what will encourage respondents to play along? Handing out sheets as people leave or sending them an email a week later provides a very weak invitation to participate. Some of the ideas suggested as 'live feedback' above and the examples noted in Table 13.2 create an invitation that is more likely to involve a greater number of people. If they have to turn their feedback into a cannonball or paper plane and throw it, the invitation is simple (anyone can screw up a ball and attempt a throw), communal (once the most engaged start throwing, others will join in) and playful. Think about a range of options that provide different invitations to get involved and decide which option(s) provide the widest and easiest invitation for the participants.

Limitations and Criticisms of Playful Feedback Tools

In the first section of this chapter I explored some of the issues of generating feedback that might be biased towards positive outcomes. Making activities fun and enjoyable can be perceived as a means to enhance the emotional states of respondents at the time of providing feedback. This is a potential bias that needs to be discussed, potentially with stakeholders that have an interest in the outcomes (such as those funding events). The personality of some events may be more suited to more playful approaches to gaining feedback. An event with a particularly serious theme or personality may of course be inappropriate for such approaches; indeed, the sudden introduction of playfulness right at the end as a sharp contrast could be viewed as artificial and inappropriate. This is both a design and value judgement that lies with the organisers and other stakeholders.

Interpretation of playfully acquired feedback needs context. There may be a need to gain multiple types of feedback, such as discussions, online views, smile sheet ratings. The number and nature of the multiple modes of feedback will depend on how the outcomes are to be used. Different 'voices' provide more context, as do greater numbers of people reporting. The feedback itself may be viewed as trivialised due to the mode of acquisition. There is a potential tension between playful evaluation or behaviours of organisers and the seriousness that surrounds complaints and negative criticisms from participants. There needs to be opportunity for negative views to be made, potentially anonymously, and a signal that these are taken seriously within the framework of the event's management and planning. How playful a person is at any time varies, and this is complicated by differences in their recent experiences within your event.

A more balanced approach that incorporates playful feedback can be achieved by guiding those who wish to be more serious (and less pleased as customers) to avenues that they will feel comfortable in reporting through. After the event, asynchronous methods may play a key role with this: the obvious tools being emails and text boxes available after the event. Communicating this aspect while retaining a playful atmosphere can be tricky, and this will need to be considered in advance of the feedback element. The associated communications can stress that there is an understanding that the playful approach 'is not for everyone', and an inclusive and professional undertone may be needed. These are all value judgements for the organiser and will depend greatly on the type and personality of the event.

Processing, Interpreting and Sharing Playfully Collected Feedback

There are many views and approaches to analysing and presenting the outcomes of surveys. I do not intend to outline here any complex principles behind quantitative or qualitative analyses and the accompanying modes of presentation of such outcomes. I do however want to raise the question of whether the outcomes are shared and reported in a playful way. As has been flagged, this depends to a great deal on the purposes and audience for the outcomes. If you are preparing a document that is being appraised by a funding body, then a pirate theme may not be the most appropriate format for your overview. However, if you are feeding back to participants or your event is to be viewed in the context of its personality/theme that is playful, then you may want to carry that theme through to the reporting.

The simplest approaches would be to utilise the language, images and personality of the feedback acquisition tools. The same design from the survey sheets and presentations could be included in summaries. You may build in caveats to justify the approaches, perhaps based on the notions of higher response rates and a wish to move away from the norm to avoid survey fatigue. In our pirate example, frequencies of responses may be visualised as differing amounts of pirate treasure rather than pie charts and comments may be contextualised as treasure found or walking the plank.

Case Study 36: LEGO Serious Play™ for reflection (Alex Moseley)

LEGO Serious Play™ was used to facilitate the final session of a research conference involving all 45 participants. The session took place over the course of one hour, with attendees sat in groups of six around tables.

The session had two aims: first, to allow attendees to reflect on their conference experience and apply elements to their own practice; and second, to counter the usual 'slump' at the end of a conference where people drift away (mentally and physically).

Using a LEGO Serious Play™ methodology, a series of question-build-share activities were set up as follows:

1   Build a simple LEGO model (from instructions) to practice building.
2   Modify that model to show how you currently feel (at the end of the conference).
3   Build a new model to show the best new thing you discovered or thought at the conference.
4   Build a new model to represent yourself having implemented all the new things you discovered at the conference.

For each step, everyone built a model as described and then explained it to the others on their table. Models are metaphors, rather than real representations, so that feelings, emotions and ideas can be included. Everyone gets to share and explain their model; others on the table all listen. Attendees were engaged throughout, and there was lively discussion and activity across the room. Tables managed themselves well, with the facilitator able to move between the tables to provide building advice and encouragement.

At the end of the session, participants could take a photograph of their final model to keep as a reminder, but it would be useful to have a more permanent reminder that could stay visible when attendees returned to their desks. They could either keep the LEGO model or maybe write a short summary of their description on a postcard to accompany the image. The session worked well for this number of people and one facilitator; the session would work with larger groups, but further facilitators would be needed.

Conclusion

Getting meaningful feedback from event participants can be challenging. I suggest that playful approaches can enhance response rates, add a flavour of fun to events and challenge the 'positive bias' in much existing evaluation. There are many ways to get participant feedback, and I have explored a range of approaches to build on existing techniques as a means to give this component of events management a new lease on life.

The approaches used should be relevant to the personality of an event. A value judgement about whether playful approaches are appropriate needs to be made by the organisers and any stakeholders who have an interest in the outcomes. There are many considerations, in terms of when, how and why the feedback is collected and then reported. For illustration I used a simple pirate theme here, but there is a wealth of other themes appropriate to different events. Ultimately, it is up to the reader to decide if playful evaluation is akin to buried treasure or if getting on board could lead to walking the plank.

Part VI
Conclusion

14 Future Play

Nicola Whitton and Alex Moseley

Introduction

Drawing on our collective experiences of play, and in particular of designing and running the Playful Learning conference over the past three years, the previous chapters have shared our experiences and insights in a number of key areas. We looked at how to design playful experiences by drawing on theory; the 'big picture' of planning an event and dealing with organisational politics; and the importance of appreciating that different audiences have different needs and will have different attitudes towards play. In the third part of the book, we considered the importance of creating safe playful spaces and approaches to doing this with playful interludes, playful training and the day-to-day management of successful playful experiences. The fourth part looked at how to engage participants in playful events by exploring different ways in which immersion can provide high engagement for group events, the potential of collaborating with external partners and approaches to designing full conference games. In the final core section, we considered ways of incorporating play into practice by making presentations more playful using a range of playful technologies and non-digital tools and ways of evaluating events playfully.

Finally, in this concluding chapter, we will revisit some of the key themes that emerged throughout the book: looking first at the diversity of play and many different motivations to play. One aspect that has come through in many of the chapters is the importance of understanding these motivations in order to engage different people in play. It is crucial also to recognise that play is a privilege and not necessarily open to all, and to consider ways to counter this and make it accessible. We consider what a future research agenda for playful learning events might look like and conclude by revising the core pillars of the Playful Learning conference and exploring how these might be applied more broadly.

There are Many Ways to Play

There is now a wider variety of different ways in which people can play, and perceptions of what is – and what is not – considered to be a play activity are subjective. In particular, we described the different ways in which adults play in Chapter 2, although many adult players (by our broad definition) may not consider themselves as such. The notion that play is, by its very nature, frivolous and purposeless does not take account of the wide variety of types of play and the variety of effects (and outcomes) that playfulness can lead to. In order to take account of the wide variety of forms of play, play activities could be considered to form a continuum, say from the 'profound' to the 'profane'. At one end are the deeply serious, solemn or ritualistic forms of play (e.g. high-level chess, battle re-enactment, professional football, gambling), and at the other the highly ludic, autotelic and visceral forms (e.g. sex play, bungee jumping, escape rooms).

Play means many different things to many people and it is important to recognise its many forms. It can be social, but it can also be solitary. It can be silly but also serious. Play is infinite in its variety.

There are Lots of Reasons to Play

Understanding how and why different people play is key to getting the most out of playful approaches. In this book we have considered the different ways in which people play and the importance of taking account of this variety. For some people and forms of play, the joy will be in the play act itself and the motivation purely intrinsic; in other circumstances play may have a strong extrinsic motivator (e.g. an external reward such as money or status, or the function of the play activity beyond its own sake, such as facilitating social interaction or killing time). The subjective nature of play makes a definition of play that lies with an activity difficult: the same activity engaged in by two different people at different times may have entirely different motivations. For this reason, we think it is more useful to focus on playfulness – the attitude of the individual engaging in the activity – rather than whether an individual activity is play. Playful learning is about encouraging and facilitating a playful approach (and associated attitudes towards risk, failure and innovation) rather than simply using tools such as games. The approach also overcomes one of the issues surrounding the language of play in that words such as 'play', 'game' or 'toy' will immediately alienate those participants who do not see play as appropriate. Using qualifiers such as 'serious' might decrease these negative attitudes but undermine the real value of playfulness – its very lack of seriousness. Using playful learning approaches neatly sidesteps the issue – it is easy to be playful without ever having to explicitly tell participants you are doing so.

In practice, most players are driven by a combination of both extrinsic and intrinsic motivations, and it is important to recognise this. People attending playful events have different attitudes to play and motivations for engaging that are exhibited by those that attend events, and it is important to consider how to engage a spectrum of more or less playful people. It is important also to remember that play is always collaborative; even when competition is involved, the players collaborate to engage in the rules of play.

Play is Not Always the Answer

There are lots of ways in which we can make the world more playful, and we have described different approaches throughout this book, but not everyone is as convinced that play is beneficial or even appropriate in many cases. Throughout this book we have looked at ways in which play can be sold to the unconvinced by getting buy-in at different levels and overcoming assumptions about the nature and value of play. An ongoing theme is the importance of permission to play – both for participants in playful events and for ourselves as designers.

We must never forget, however, that play is a privilege that is not open to all, and positioning play as an inclusive practice is key to its sustainability. It is also worth remembering that playful learning approaches are not appropriate at all times or for all events, conferences and activities. Like any teaching and learning approach, it has its drawbacks and limitations and must be considered as a tool in the armoury rather than a panacea. Throughout the book, this is represented by advice and methods to allow small interventions, pilot projects or a sliding level of playfulness from light to more embedded.

The Future of Playful Learning

So what does the future hold for playful learning? It is a field that is growing both in practice and credibility, but it currently lacks a robust research foundation. On the future agenda for research and practice is a clear need for an evidence base for the benefits of play and playfulness in different contexts, disciplines and levels. While we hypothesise that there is a beneficial relationship between safe failure, managing risk, building resilience and developing true creativity and innovation – and have practical experience of these benefits through our involvement in the learning and training events described in this book – there is not yet a research foundation.

As the field grows and becomes more established, it will become increasingly important to understanding the relevance and appropriateness of play in adult education and the workplace and to evaluate the value on learning, health and well-being more widely. Establishing the best practice for playfulness as an inclusive practice is also crucial.

Conclusion

To conclude, we wanted to revisit the five pillars of the Playful Learning conference, to highlight their importance both to shape playful learning events but also as approaches to live a more playful life. A focus on **innovation** and playing with the new without fear of failure avoids the potential of being stuck in a rut and doing the same old things simply because they are safe. Maintaining a sense of **integrity** explicitly focusses on what is right and what is fair and underpins a playful philosophy with an ethical and inclusive ideology. In this field, perhaps more so than many, **rigour**, robust research practices and peer scrutiny are absolutely essential to maintain the credibility of the area. Keeping a sense of **mischief**, subversion, frivolity and delight is really at the heart of what playfulness means for us. Above all, other people are the key to a playful philosophy: play is all about the players, and **collegiality** is what makes playful learning so powerful.

References

Bateson, P. (2014). Play, Playfulness, Creativity and Innovation. *Animal Behavior and Cognition, 2*(2), 99.

Bateson, P., & Martin, P. (2013). *Play, Playfulness, Creativity and Innovation.* Cambridge: Cambridge University Press.

Boal, A. (2002). *Games for Actors and Non-Actors.* London: Routledge.

Bogost, I. (2016). *Play Anything: The Pleasure of Limits, the Uses of Boredom, and the Secret of Games.* New York: Basic Books.

Bratton, S. C., Ray, D., Rhine, T., & Jones, L. (2005). The Efficacy of Play Therapy With Children. *Professional Psychology: Research and Practice, 36*(4), 376–390.

Brown, S., & Vaughan, C. (2010). *Play: How It Shapes the Brain, Opens the Imagination, and Invigorates the Soul.* New York, NY: Penguin.

Burton, W. B., Civitano, A., & Steiner-Grossman, P. (2012). Online Versus Paper Evaluations: Differences in both Quantitative and Qualitative Data. *Journal of Computing in Higher Education, 24*(1), 58–69.

Buys, N., & Bursnall, S. (2007). Establishing University–Community Partnerships: Processes and Benefits. *Journal of Higher Education Policy and Management, 29*(1), 73–86.

Caillois, R., & Barash, M. (2001). *Man, Play, and Games.* Champaign, IL: University of Illinois Press.

Calleja, G. (2011). *In-Game: From Immersion to Incorporation.* Cambridge, MA: MIT Press.

Carifio, J., & Perla, R. (2008). Resolving the 50-year Debate around Using and Misusing Likert Scales. *Medical Education, 42*(12), 1150–1152.

Carse, J. P. (1986). *Finite and Infinite Games: A Vision of Life as Play and Possibilities.* New York: Ballantine.

Carter, A. J., Croft, A., Lukas, D., & Sandstrom, G. M. (2018). Women's Visibility in Academic Seminars: Women Ask Fewer Questions than Men. *PLoS ONE, 13*(9).

Colarusso, C. A. (1993). Play in Adulthood: A Developmental Consideration. *Psychoanalytic Study of the Child, 48,* 225–245.

Csikszentmihalyi, M. (1992). *Flow: The Classic Work on How to Achieve Happiness.* London: Random House.

De Koven, B. (1978). *The Well-Played Game: A Player's Philosophy.* Garden City, NY: Anchor Books.

De Koven, B. (2014). *A Playful Path.* Pittsburgh, PA: ECT Press.

Deterding, S. (2018). Alibis for Adult Play: A Goffmanian Account of Escaping Embarrassment in Adult Play. *Games and Culture, 13*(3), 260–279.

Egenfeldt-Nielsen, S., Smith, J. H., & Tosca, S. P. (2008). *Understanding Video Games: The Essential Introduction*. New York: Routledge.

Eggleston, T., & Smith, G. (2004). *Building Community in the Classroom through Ice-Breakers and Parting Ways*. Washington, DC.

Flanagan, M. (2009). *Critical Play: Radical Game Design*. Cambridge, MA: MIT Press.

Glenn, P., & Knapp, M. (1987). The Interactive Framing of Play in Adult Conversations. *Communication Quarterly*, *31*(5), 48–66.

Goffman, E. (1959). *The Presentation of Self in Everyday Life*. New York: Anchor Books.

Goffman, E. (1967). *Interaction Ritual: Essays in Face-to-Face Behavior*. New York: Doubleday.

Goffman, E. (1986). *Frame Analysis: An Essay on the Organization of Experience*. Boston, MA: Northeastern University Press.

Graetz, K. A., & Goliber, M. J. (2002). Designing Collaborative Learning Places: Psychological Foundations and New Frontiers. *New Directions in Teaching and Learning*, *92*, 13–11.

Guitard, P., Ferland, F., & Dutil, É. (2005). Toward a Better Understanding of Playfulness in Adults. *The Occupational Therapy Journal of Research (OTJR): Occupation, Participation and Health*, *25*(1), 9–22.

Harviainen, J. T. (2012). Ritualistic Games, Boundary Control, and Information Uncertainty. *Simulation & Gaming*, *43*(4), 506–527.

Huizinga, J. (1955). *Homo Ludens: A Study of the Play Element in Culture*. Boston: Beacon Press.

Jones, R., & Shields, E. (2018). Using Games to Disrupt the Conference Twitter-sphere, *26*(1063519), 1–10.

Jones, R., Peters, K., & Shields, E. (2007). Transform your Training: Practical Approaches to Interactive Information Literacy Teaching. *Journal of Information Literacy*, *1*(1).

Juul, J. (2013). *The Art of Failure: An Essay on the Pain of Playing Video Games*. Cambridge, MA: MIT Press.

Kalir, J.H., Fahy, M., Kupperman, J., Schiff, F.M., & Stanzler, J. (2018). Playful Partnerships for Game-Based Learning in International Contexts. In I. Lubin (Ed.), *ICT-Supported Innovations in Small Countries and Developing Regions* (pp. 141–168). Berlin: Springer.

Kavanagh, M., Clark-Murphy, M., & Wood, L. (2011). The First Class: Using Icebreakers to Facilitate Transition in a Tertiary Environment. *Asian Social Science*, *7*(4), 84–92.

Krosnick, J. A., Holbrook, A. L., Berent, M. K., Carson, R. T., Hanemann, W. M., Kopp, R. J., ... Conaway, M. (2002). The Impact of "No Opinion" Response Options on Data Quality. *Public Opinion Quarterly*, *66*(3), 371–403.

Kultima, A., Alha, K., & Nummenmaa, T. (2016). Design Constraints in Game Design. Case: Survival Mode Game Jam 2016. In *Proceedings of the International Conference on Game Jams, Hackathons, and Game Creation Events – GJH&GC '16* (pp. 22–29). New York, NY: ACM.

Langan, A. M., Scott, N., Partington, S., Oczujda, A., Langan, A. M., Scott, N., & Partington, S. (2017). Coherence between Text Comments and the Quantitative Ratings in the UK's National Student Survey. *Journal of Further and Higher Education*, *14*(1), 1–14.

Lieberman, N. (1977). *Playfulness: Its Relationship to Imagination and Creativity.* New York: Academic Press.

Lillemyr, O. F. (2009). *Taking Play Seriously: Children and Play in Early Childhood Education – An Exciting Challenge.* Charlotte, NC: Information Age Publishing.

Lockwood, R., & O'Connor, S. (2017). Playfulness in Adults: An Examination of Play and Playfulness and their Implications for Coaching. *Coaching, 10*(1), 54–65.

Lopata, C., Wallace, N. V., & Finn, K. V. (2005). Comparison of Academic Achievement Between Montessori and Traditional Education Programs. *Journal of Research in Childhood Education, 20*(1).

Malone, T. W. (1980). *What Makes Things Fun to Learn? A Study of Intrinsically Motivating Computer Games.* Palo Alto, California: Xerox.

Maniaci, M. R., & Rogge, R. D. (2014). Caring about Carelessness: Participant Inattention and its Effects on Research. *Journal of Research in Personality, 48*(1), 61–83.

Montola, M., Stenros, J., & Waern, A. (2009). *Pervasive Games: Theory and Design (Morgan Kaufmann Game Design Books).* Burlington, MA:CRC Press.

Moseley, A. (2013). Assessment: A Case for Integration in T. Connolly et al. (Eds.), *Psychology, Pedagogy and Assessment in Serious Games.* Hershey, PA: IGI Global, 342–356.

Moseley, A., & Whitton, N. (2015). *Playful Learning: Using Games to Enhance the Student Experience.* York, Hershey, PA: Higher Education Academy.

Nielsen, J. (2006). *The 90-9-1 Rule for Participation Inequality in Social Media and Online Communities.* Blog post, 9 October 2006. Available: https://www.nngroup.com/articles/participation-inequality/

Noland, C., & Penny, S. (2014). Embodiment. In M. Kelly (Ed.), *Encyclopedia of Aesthetics.* (2nd ed.) Oxford: Oxford University Press.

Nørgård, R., Toft-Nielsen, C., & Whitton, N. (2017). Playful Learning in Higher Education: Developing a Signature Pedagogy. *International Journal of Play, 6*(3).

Oliver, P. V., & Weinswig, S. E. (1996). *The Human Scavenger Hunt: A Unique Classroom Ice-Breaker Exercise.* Hartford, CT.

Owens, D., Davis, A., Murphy, J. D., Khazanchi, D., & Zigurs, I. (2009). Real-World Opportunities for Virtual – World Project Management. *IT Professional, 11*(2), 34–41.

Owler, K., Morrison, R., & Plester, B. (2010). Does Fun Work? The Complexity of Promoting Fun at Work. *Journal of Management & Organization, 16*(3), 338–352.

Pedler, M. (2011). Leadership, Risk and the Imposter Syndrome. *Action Learning: Research and Practice, 8*(2), 89–91.

Peterson, C., & Seligman, M. (2004). *Character Strengths and Virtues: A Handbook and Classification.* Oxford: Oxford University Press.

Peterson, R. A., & Wilson, W. R. (1992). Measuring Customer Satisfaction: Fact and Artifact. *Journal of the Academy of Marketing Science, 20*(1), 61–71.

Phillips, J. J., Breining, M. T., & Phillips, P. P. (2008). *Return on Investment in Meetings and Events: Tools and Techniques to Measure the Success of All Types of Meetings and Events.* New York: Routledge.

Podsakoff, P. M., MacKenzie, S. B., Lee, J. Y., & Podsakoff, N. P. (2003). Common Method Biases in Behavioral Research: A Critical Review of the Literature and Recommended Remedies. *Journal of Applied Psychology, 88*(5), 879–903.

Proyer, R. T. (2011). Being Playful and Smart? The Relations of Adult Playfulness with Psychometric and Self-Estimated Intelligence and Academic Performance. *Learning and Individual Differences*, *21*(4), 463–467.

Proyer, R. T. (2013). The Well-Being of Playful Adults: Adult Playfulness, Subjective Well-Being, Physical Well-Being, and the Pursuit of Enjoyable Activities. *The European Journal of Humour Research*, *1*(1), 84–98.

Proyer, R. T. (2014). Playfulness Over the Lifespan and its Relation to Happiness. *Zeitschrift Für Gerontologie Und Geriatrie*, *47*(6), 508–512.

Remmele, B., & Whitton, N. (2014). Disrupting the Magic Circle: The Impact of Negative Social Gaming Behaviours. In T. M. Connolly, L. Boyle, T. Hainey, G. Baxter, & P. Moreno-Ger (Eds.), *Psychology, Pedagogy and Assessment in Serious Games* (pp. 111–126). Hershey, PA: IGI Global.

Riva, G., Mantovani, F., Capideville, C. S., Preziosa, A., Morganti, F., Villani, D., … Alcañiz, M. (2007). Affective Interactions Using Virtual Reality: The Link between Presence and Emotions. *CyberPsychology and Behaviour*, *10*(1).

Ross, L. F., Loup, A., Nelson, R. M., Botkin, J. R., Kost, R., Smith, G. R., & Gehlert, S. (2010). The Challenges of Collaboration for Academic and Community Partners in a Research Partnership: Points to Consider. *Journal of Empirical Research on Human Research Ethics*, *5*(1), 19–31.

Salen, K., & Zimmerman, E. (2004). *Rules of Play: Game Design Fundamentals*. Cambridge, MA: The MIT Press.

Schell, J. (2008). *The Art of Game Design: A Book of Lenses*. Boca Raton, FL: CRC Press.

Schwarz, N., & Clore, G. L. (1983). Mood, Misattribution, and Judgements of Well-Being: Informative and Directive Functions of Affective States. *Journal of Personality and Social Psychology*, *45*(3), 513–523.

Sicart, M. (2014). *Play Matters*. Cambridge, MA: MIT Press.

Statler, M., Roos, J., & Victor, B. (2009). Ain't Misbehavin': Taking Play Seriously in Organizations. *Journal of Change Management*, *9*(1), 87–107.

Suits, B. (1978). *The Grasshopper: Games, Life and Utopia*. Peterborough, Canada: Broadview Press.

Sutton-Smith, B. (1997). *The Ambiguity of Play*. Cambridge, MA: Harvard University Press.

Tuckman, B. (1965). Developmental Sequence in Small Groups. *Psychological Bulletin*, *63*(6), 384–399.

Tum, J., Norton, P., & Wright, J. (2006). *Management of Event Operations*. Oxford: Butterworth-Heinemann/Elsevier.

Turner, P., & Turner, S. (2006). Place, Sense of Place and Presence. *Presence: Teleoperators and Virtual Environments*, *15*(2), 204–217.

Vygotsky, L. S. (1978). *Mind in Society: Development of Higher Psychological Processes*. Cambridge, MA: Harvard University Press.

Walsh, A. (2017). *Making Escape Rooms for Educational Purposes: A Workbook*. Tallin, EU: Innovative Libraries.

Whitton, N. (2005). Designing Effective Icebreakers for Online Community Building. In *Proceedings of ALT-C 2005*. Oxford: Association for Learning Technology.

Whitton, N. (2007). *An Investigation into the Potential of Collaborative Computer Game-Based Learning in Higher Education*. Edinburgh: Edinburgh Napier University.

Whitton, N. (2014). *Digital Games and Learning: Research and Theory*. New York, NY: Routledge.

Whitton, N. (2018). Playful Learning: Tools, Techniques, and Tactics. *Research in Learning Technology, 26*. https://doi.org/10.25304/rlt.v26.2035

Wiessner, C. A., Hatcher, T., Chapman, D., & Storberg-Walker, J. (2008). Creating New Learning at Professional Conferences: An Innovative Approach to Conference Learning, Knowledge Construction and Programme Evaluation. *Human Resource Development International, 11*(4), 367–383.

Woodcock, J. (2017). *Working the Phones: Control and Resistance in Call Centres*. London, UK: Pluto Press.

Index

Game or event titles *Capitalised in Italics*
References in boxed case studies or illustrations *in italics*.